THE
STORY OF
BURKE AND HARE

By

ALEXANDER LEIGHTON

First published in 1861

Read & Co.

Copyright © 2020 Read & Co. History

This edition is published by Read & Co. History,
an imprint of Read & Co.

This book is copyright and may not be reproduced or copied in any
way without the express permission of the publisher in writing.

British Library Cataloguing-in-Publication Data
A catalogue record for this book is available
from the British Library.

Read & Co. is part of Read Books Ltd.
For more information visit
www.readandcobooks.co.uk

CONTENTS

ALEXANDER LEIGHTON

By Thomas Wilson Bayne

Editor of *Tales of the Borders*, was born at Dundee in 1800. After distinguishing himself at Dundee academy he studied medicine at Edinburgh and settled there, first working as a lawyer's clerk and then as a man of letters.

The *Tales of the Borders*, a series of short stories, still popular among the Scottish peasantry, was projected at Berwick-on-Tweed in 1834 by John Mackay Wilson, on whose death in 1835 his brother continued the work for a time. Shortly afterwards an Edinburgh publisher named Sutherland became proprietor, and Leighton was appointed editor and chief story writer; the series was completed in 1840. He received assistance from Hugh Miller, Thomas Gillespie (1777–1844), and others. Reading widely he had an extensive, if not very accurate, knowledge of many subjects, including metaphysics and especially Hume's philosophy.

He died 24 Dec. 1874.

In 1857 Leighton re-edited the complete *Tales of the Borders*, and this was reissued in 1863–4, 1869 (with additions), and in 1888. In 1860–1 he published two series of *Curious Storied Traditions of Scottish Life,* in 1864 *Mysterious Legends of Edinburgh*, in 1865 *Shellburn*, a novel, and in 1867 his interesting *Romance of the Old Town of Edinburgh.*

Other of his works are: *The Court of Cacus, Or The Story of Burke and Hare, Men and Women of History, Jephthah's Daughter, A Dictionary of Religions*, and a Latin metrical version of Burns's songs, which Carlyle praised. Various writers submitted their books to his editing, and he probably wrote whole volumes to which others prefixed their names.

A BIOGRAPHY FROM

Dictionary of National Biography, 1885-1900, *Volume* 33

PREFACE

I have not written this book,—narrating a series of tragedies unprecedented in the history of mankind, as well for the number of victims and the depth of their sufferings as for the sordid temptation of the actors,—without a proper consideration of what is due to the public and myself. If I had thought I was to contribute to the increase of a taste for moral stimulants, said to be peculiarly incident to our age—and yet, I suspect, as strong in all bygone times—and without any countervailing advantage to morals and the welfare of society, I would have desisted from my labours.

But, being satisfied that what has really occurred on the stage of the world, however involving the dignity of our nature or revolting to human feelings, must and will be known in some way, wherever there are eyes to read or ears to hear, nay, was intended to be known by Him through whose permission it was allowed to be, I consider it a benefaction that the knowledge which kills shall be accompanied by the knowledge which cures. Nay, were it possible, which it is not, to keep from succeeding generations cases of great depravity punished for example, and atoned for by penitence, the man who tried to conceal them would be acting neither in obedience to God's providence nor for the good of the people.

We know what the Bible records of the doings of depraved men, and we know also for what purpose; and may we not follow in the steps of the inspired?

But a slight survey of the nature of the mind may satisfy any one, not necessarily a philosopher, that it requires as its natural food examples of evil with the punishment and the cure. If it had been so ordered that there were not in the soil of the heart congenital germs of wickedness ready to spring up and branch into crimes under favouring circumstances, which the complications of society are eternally producing, and that, consequently, all evil was sheer imitation, something might be said for concealing the thing to be imitated, even at the expense of losing the antidote. Even in that case the "huddlers-up" would not be very philosophical or very sensible; religious they could not be, because the supposition is adverse to the most fundamental truth of Christianity—for, as the imitation must of necessity be admitted to be catching, where so many are caught, the deterring influences would be more necessary. But as all must admit that the evil comes of itself and the antidote from man, those who would conceal the latter must allow to the former its full sway.

In all this, I do not overlook the benefits of abstract representations of the beauty of virtue and the ugliness of vice. These belong to the department of the imagination, where no principle of action resides; and every one knows that the images must be embodied, in particular instances taken from the real world of flesh and blood, so that the historian of real occurrences must still work as an adjunct even to the fancy. If it be said that he narrates stories that are revolting, the answer would seem to be that, as the law still justifies example, and society calls for it, the objection that the interest of a story is *too deep* can only be used by those who view the records of wickedness as a stimulant and not as a terror, or those who, amidst the still-recurring daily murders, consider society as beyond the need of amendment. The objection is thus an adjection.

Fortunately, none of us are acquainted with *amiable* enormities, and the longer these remain unknown to us, the better for us and mankind; so that it seems to follow, that he who can render the acted crimes of history as disagreeable and hateful as they can be made, even with the aid of the dark shadows of his fancy, performs an act favourable to the interests of society. Yet I have done my best to save from revolt the feelings of the virtuous, as far as is consistent with the moral effect intended by Providence to be produced on the vicious.

YORK LODGE, TRINITY, *September 1861.*

FIRST APPEARANCE
IN SURGEON'S SQUARE

When the gloaming was setting in of an evening in the autumn of 1827, and when the young students of Dr Knox's class had covered up those remains of their own kind from which they had been trying to extract nature's secrets, one was looking listlessly from the window into the Square. The place was as quiet as usual, silent and sad enough to gratify a fancy that there existed some connexion between the stillness and the work carried on from day to day and night to night in these mysterious recesses; for, strange enough, whatever curiosity might be felt by the inhabitants as to what was done there, few were ever seen within that area except those in some way connected with the rooms. So was it the more likely that our young student's eye should have been attracted by the figure of a man moving stealthily under the shade of the houses. Then he looked more intently to ascertain whether he was not one of the regular staff of body-snatchers who supplied "the thing," as they called it. But no; the stranger, whoever he might be, was neither "Merryandrew," nor "the Spune," nor "the Captain," nor any other of the gouls,—some half-dozen,—yet he would have done no discredit to the fraternity either as to dress or manner: little and thick-set, with a firm round face, small eyes, and Irish nose, a down-looking sleazy dog, who, as he furtively turned his eye up to the window, seemed to think he had no right to direct his vision beyond the parallel of a man's pocket.

The student, who could dissect living character no less than he could dead tissue, immediately suspected that this meditative "worshipper of the sweets of eve" was there upon business, but, being probably new to the calling, he was timid, if not bashful. Yes, bashful; we do not retract the word, comely as it is, for where, in all this wide world of sin and shamelessness, could we suppose it possible to find a man who lives upon it, and is shone on by its sun, and cheered by its flowers, capable of selling the body of his fellow-creature for gold without having his face suffused with blood, cast up by the indignant heart, at least for the first time? And perhaps it was the first time to this new-comer. But in whatever condition the strange man might be, the student had got over *his* weakness, that is, nature's strength, and, resolving to test the lounger, he went down, and, shewing himself at the door, beckoned the bashful one forward.

"Were you looking for any one?" said he, as he peered into the down-looking face, where there never had been a blush.

"'Mph!—are you Dr Knox?"

"No; but I am one of his students," was the reply of the young man, who was now nearly satisfied of the intention of the stranger.

"And, sure, I'm not far wrong thin, afther all."

"And I may suit your purpose as well, perhaps."

"Perhaps."

"Well, speak out; don't be afraid. Have you got 'the thing?'"

"Doun't know what you mean."

"Ah! not an old hand, I perceive. You were never here before?"

"No."

"And don't know what to say?"

"No."

And the bashful man again turned his gloomy eyes to the ground, and didn't know what to do with those hands of his, which were not made for kid—perhaps for skin of another kind. And shouldn't this hardened student have been sorry for a man in such confusion; but he wasn't—nay, he had no sympathy with his refinement.

"Why, man, don't you speak out?" he said impatiently.

"There's some one coming through the Square there," was the

12

reply, as the man looked furtively to a side.

"Come in here, then," said the student, as he pulled him into a large room where there were three young men who acted as Knox's assistants.

And there they were in the midst of a great number of coarse tables, with one large one in the middle, whereon were deposited—each having its portion—masses or lumps of some matter which could not be seen by reason of all of them being covered with pieces of cloth—once white, but now dirty gray, as if they had been soiled with clammy hands for weeks or months. Nor were these signs, though unmistakeable to even the neophyte, all that there spoke with a terrible eloquence of man's lowly destiny upon earth; ay, and of man's pride too, even that pride of science which makes such a fool of him in the very midst of the evidences of his corruption; for although the windows were opened a little way, the choking air, thick with gases which, in other circumstances, the free wind carries off to dissipate and purify in the storm, pressed heavily upon the lungs, so that even the uninitiated shrank with unfeigned feeling, as if he shuddered under an awe that was perfectly foreign to his rough nature.

"Sure, and I'm among the dead," said the man, whom the reader will have discovered to be an Irishman; "and I have something ov that kind to——"

"Sell," added one assistant sharply, as, in his scientific ardour, he anticipated the merchant.

"Yes."

And now the bashful man was relieved of his burden of shame, light or heavy as you please; but we verily say of *some* weight, as we have him at the beginning of a career which made the world ring till the echoes might have disturbed the gods, and we know that he was not otherwise without feelings pertaining to humanity; nay, we know, and shall tell, that on one occasion pity suffused an eye that was destined to be oftener and longer red with the fires of cruelty than was ever before in the world's history the orb of a human being.

"And what do you give for *wun*?" he whispered, as he sidled up to the ear of the young anatomist who had been speaking to him.

"Sometimes as high as £10."

And for certain, if the student had been curious enough to estimate the effect of such words upon such a man, to whom "ten pennies" would have been words of inspiration, he would have seen in that eye, no longer dull and muddy, the first access of that demon mammon, as by the touch upon the heart it raised the first pulses of a fever which was to grow and grow, till it dried up into a parched and senseless thing the fountain of pity; for, however inoperative, we are bound to say it was still there, as if abiding God's judgments—and transform one nature altogether into another—*for a purpose.*

"And wouldn't you give a pound more for a fresh wun?" said he, with that intoxication of hope which sometimes makes a beggar play with a new-born fortune.

"Sometimes more and sometimes less," replied the other; "but 'the thing' must always be seen."

"And by my sowl it is a good thing, and worth the money any how."

"Where is it?"

"At home."

"Then if you will bring it here about ten it will be examined, and you will get your money; and since you are a beginner, I may tell you, you had better bring it in a box."

"And have we not a tea-chest all ready, which howlds it nate, and will not my friend help me to bring it?"

"Well, mind the hour, and be upon your guard that no one sees you."

And so the man, however much an adult in the common immorality of the world, in this singular crime as yet an infant, left to complete his sale of merchandise. It would not be easy to figure his thoughts,—perhaps more difficult to estimate his feelings,—yet it might be for good that we could analyse these states of the mind, which are nought other than diseases, that we might apply the cure which God has vouchsafed to our keeping; even as that student strove to inquire into the secrets of the body, that he might learn how to deal with the living frame when it is out of order, or, perhaps, hastening to a premature dissolution.

That man was William Burke, and we say this as a historian might have said, that man was Alexander of Macedon, or that Julius Caesar, or that Napoleon—all equally great, or at least great with the difference that the first *as yet* only desecrated the temple for money, and the others took from it the deity for ambition. Ay, and with this difference also, which time was to shew, that while there have been many slaughtering kings, there never was but one William Burke.

INTERCALARY

The ardour of the study of anatomy was in the youth, and it was there from sympathy; yea, for years before, the Square and the College had been under the fervour of competition. Nor was this fervour limited to the Scottish metropolis, from which the fame of the successive Monroes had gone forth over the world. There had arisen Barclay, who, as an extra-academical lecturer, had the faculty of inspiring his students with all the zeal which he himself possessed, and to his class in the Square there had come students from England and Ireland, as well as foreign parts. Even in prior times, when the teaching was almost limited to the college, the reputation of the professors had so accumulated *élèves* that Scotland groaned, and groaned ineffectually, under the invasion of her sacred graveyards. The country teemed with stories, in which there figured the midnight adventures of those strange men who gained a living by supplying, at all hazards, what was so peremptorily required in the scientific hall and its adjacent rooms.[1] Anxious mourners visited by the light of the moon the places where their dear relatives lay entombed, as if they could thereby satisfy themselves that the beloved bodies still rested there in peace, though it was certain that the artists became in a short time so proficient in their work that they could leave a grave apparently as entire as it was at the time when the mourners deposited their burden. That these adventures should have taken strange and sometimes grimly-ludicrous turns might have been expected, and yet it is more true that they transcended belief.

There was one long current in Leven in Fife of a character more like fiction than truth. A middle-aged man of the name of Henderson had died of an acute fever, and was buried in due time. He left a widow and daughter, and we need not speak, even to those who have not experienced such privation, of the deep valley of grief through which it takes so long a time for the light of a living hope to penetrate, if, in some instances, it ever penetrates at all. Yet people must live, and the widow was to keep the small public-house in the skirts of the town which her husband had conducted. Six days had passed since the funeral, when one night, at a late hour, two men asked and got admittance for the purpose of refreshment, one of them, according to their statement, having been taken ill. They were introduced through a dark lobby into a room, where there was one of those close beds so common in Scotland, and left there with the drink they had ordered. By and by a loud knock came to the door, and the voice of an officer demanded to know if some thieves who had broken into a neighbouring house had there taken refuge. The noise and the impending search had reached the ears of the two men who had entered shortly before, and having had some good reason for being afraid of justice, they took advantage of a window and got out, but they had made so much noise in their flight, that the officers were directed to a pursuit, in which, however, they ultimately failed. On their return they thought of examining the room, with a view to ascertain whether the supposed thieves had left in their hurry any of the booty; but all that they found was an empty bag, which they took away with them for the purpose of an expected identification. The confusion having ceased, the widow, in the depth of her grief for her departed husband, went into the room to betake herself to bed. She approached it for the purpose of folding it down, and in an instant was transfixed; before her on the bed lay the dead body of her husband in those very grave-clothes made by her own hands, and in which, six days before, he had been buried. The explanation of the mystery was not difficult. The two men belonged to the College staff of body-snatchers; they had succeeded so far in their enterprise, and would with their burden have avoided all houses, if one of them had not been taken ill, and the other had not also wanted to participate in a restorative after their night's work. It is supposed that, thinking themselves secure in the quiet house, they had taken the body out of the sack for some purpose only known to themselves, and thinking, when the noise got up, that the pursuit was after them, they had flung it into the close bed and flown.

Once upon a track of such grim romance, so rich in specimens of a bypast phase of society, it is not easy to get rid of it, nor is it any more wrong to pursue it so far, to shew our social ameliorations, than it is to search for underlying strata in the physical world, which tell us of a rudeness in Nature's workings from which she progresses to more perfect organisms. Another of these stories is scarcely less interesting. A young student of the name of Burns saw one day on the big centre-table of the College practical hall what he considered to be the body of his mother. Rendered wild by the conviction, he flew out of the room, took a ticket for Dumfries, and, on arriving there, told his father (who, half-dead in grief, was confined to bed,) his terrible story. It was night, and the snow had been falling during the day, so that the graveyard was covered nearly a foot in depth, and one might have thought that the father would have put off the execution of a resolution, to which he came on the instant, of examining the grave, till the following day; but without saying a word, he rose deliberately, as if some new energy had seized him and restored him to the active duties of life, and betaking himself, accompanied by his son, to the place of sepulture, roused the sexton to the work of investigation. The lantern and the spade were put in requisition, and with the father and son as mute spectators, the green sod was removed and the mould shovelled out till the coffin was laid bare. Then the lid was unscrewed and taken off, and there lay, exposed to the eyes of the husband and the son, the body of the endeared one—the centre once of so many loves, and the source of so many domestic joys—calm in the stillness of death.

We have even a little poetry in some of these almost

innumerable stories of a state of social polity that will never return again. One was a favourite of the students about 1818. One, George Duncan, from Angus, lodged in the Potterow with another of the name of Ferguson from a shire further north. They were both in love with a Miss Wilson, who resided somewhere about Bruntsfield Links; and so embittered were they by this feeling of rivalship, that they slept together, and ate their meals together, and walked and talked together, without ever the name of the girl being mentioned by either. There seemed to be a tacit admission that each knew that the other was in love with the same individual, and that each supposed the other the favourite, and that each hated the other with all the virulence of an unsuccessful competitor. In this strange state of things between two who had once been loving friends, Ferguson died of a disease the nature of which baffled the acuteness of the best surgeons, and in the course of a few days Duncan's rival was consigned to a grave in the Buccleuch burying-ground. And now comes a far more singular part of the story. Duncan, in league with a noted snatcher at that time, called the "Screw," from the adroit way in which he managed the extracting instrument, repaired, on the second night after the funeral, to the cemetery where poor Ferguson had been deposited, with a view to lifting the body and carrying it to Dr Monro's room. It was late, and the moon shed more abundantly than the adventurers wished her soft light over the still graves, and especially that of him whose nineteenth summer sun had shown in a succession, with small interval, the smile of beauty and the grin of death. But if this poetry of nature did not affect the rival and the anatomist, something else did; for as the two slouched behind one of the grave-stones to conceal themselves till the glare of the moon should be hidden in a welcome cloud, who should be seen there, wrapped in a night-cloak, and hanging over the grave of Ferguson, but the object of their mutual affection? Nay, so near were they, that they heard her sobs and her ejaculations of "Henry, dear Henry," and many others of those soft endearments with which the heart of grief is so eloquent. If the iron had entered into Duncan's soul before, it now burned there in the red fire of his hatred. The sobbing figure rose and vanished, as do the night-visions of these places, so suggestive of flitting images, and within an hour the body of Ferguson was extended on the table within the College. Nor does the story end with this terrible satisfaction, for Duncan more than once afterwards, in the moonlit nights, witnessed from the same hiding-place, and with what satisfaction to his relentless soul may be guessed, the same offerings of the poor girl's affection over an empty grave.

And so forth, through all the number of such stories as used to be rife at that time, but have now died away amidst narratives of a more living interest. But towards the close of Barclay's labours, in his class the materials for such were rather on the increase, for the reason that the invasions on consecrated places kept a proportion to the requirements of an increasing class of students. Nor, when Barclay ceased to lecture, and was succeeded by Knox, did this Scotch shame undergo any diminution, if it did not wax more brazen in its features. Knox was destined, as well by his powers as a public lecturer as by his ambition and vindictive impatience of an intruder on his peculiar walk, and independently altogether of the dark suspicions which rose like thick exhalations out of the depths of the great tragedy subsequently enacted, to become a marked man, and the centre of attraction to ardent students. His ambition felt, too, the quickening spur of Liston, who, as an extra-academical lecturer on surgery, offered for even more than a national reputation. The professional emulation of these men soon degenerated into professional, if not personal hatred, scarcely alleviated by the collateral envy they both bore towards the academical professor, who, himself a good anatomist of the old school, with family honours not distinguished from a professional inheritance, could afford to view the new men with an easy if not proud disregard.

With these feelings among the lecturers, we may easily

fancy the almost natural effects among the students, always remarkable for devotion to their teachers. The spirit of the latter went through them like an inoculation, and, while working in them as a rancour, it took the form, as in the elders, of a professional emulation. Nay, it seemed to become almost a frenzy among them, that those of one class should excel those of another in the knowledge of the human body. Questions came to be discussed among them, often suggested by faults imputed by one lecturer to another, and the quarrels of the masters thus became bones of contention among their scholars. An unsuccessful operation would be seized on as a pretext to run down the operator; and as the anatomical books could not always, or often, settle the dispute, the area of controversy would be in the halls of dissection. In this state of affairs, it behoved that the demand for subjects, which ever since the advent of Barclay had been on the increase, should become day by day more clamant, and the number of vagabonds who betook themselves to the calling came soon to take on the form and organisation of a regular staff.

Unfortunately the characters of the leaders, with the exception of Monro, were not calculated to temper this zeal with discretion, or throw a veil of decency over the transactions of low men, which, however justified, as many said, by the necessities of science, were hostile to the instincts of nature, and fearfully resented by the feelings of relatives. Liston was accused, whether justly or not, of wiling patients from the Infirmary, to set off by his brilliant operations the imperfections of the regular surgeons of that institution; and great as he was in his profession, it is certain that he wanted that simplicity and dignity of character necessary to secure to him respect in proportion to the admiration due to his powers. But Knox was a man of a far more complex organisation, if it was indeed possible to analyse him. A despair to the physiognomist who contemplated his rough irregular countenance, with a blind eye resembling a grape, he was not less a difficulty to the psychologist. There seemed to be no principle whereby you could think of binding him down to a line of duty, and a universal sneer, not limited to mundane powers, formed the contrast to an imputed self-perfection, not without the evidence of very great scientific accomplishments. Even before he took up Barclay's class he was damaged by a story which went the round of the public, and was brought up against him at the time of his great occultation.

On returning from the Cape, where he had been attached as surgeon to a regiment, he was one day met by his old teacher, Professor Jameson, who, after a kindly recognition in his own simple way, inquired what had been his pursuits when abroad.

"Why," replied Knox, with one of these expressions of an almost unreadable face—something between a leer and overdone sincerity—"why, I was busy in your way,—keen in the study of natural history. No place in the world excels the Cape for curious objects in that department; will you believe it, Professor, I have made an extraordinary discovery?"

"Discovery! ah, you interest me."

"And well I may," he continued, as the light of the one orb expressed the new-born zeal of the naturalist. "I have found a new species of animal. Yes, sir, altogether new, and at a world's-wide distance from any congeners with which you are acquainted—quite an irreproducible phœnix."

"Then we must identify it with your name,—some adjective connected with night, but not darkness."

"And that I have done, too," continued the naturalist.

"Why, then, the description will form an excellent article for our journal. I could wish that you write it out and send it to me. It will be something grand, to shew the Southerners we are *en avant*."

"I will do it," was the reply; "and you shall have it for the next number."

Nor was Knox worse in this instance than his word, if he could be, for by and by there came to the Professor a spirited, if not elaborate description of the new species, which, having been approved of by the simple Professor, flared brilliantly among the heavy articles of his beloved work. But unhappily for the discoverer, no less than for the editor, the article fell under the eye of Dr Buckland, who soon found out the whole affair to be an excellent hoax. Often afterwards Jameson looked for his contributor to administer a reproof in his gentle way, but this opportunity never awaited him, for Knox, though with one eye, had a long sight when there was danger ahead, and the Professor in the distance sent him down the nearest close with even more than his usual celerity.

Those who knew the man would have no hesitation in placing such an example of his recklessness to the credit of his rampant egotism,[2] certainly not to that of practical joking, a species of devil's humour not always dissociated from a *bonhommie* to which the earnest mind of the man was a stranger. Even the bitterness of soul towards competitors was not sufficiently gratified by the pouring forth of the toffana-spirit of his sarcasm. He behoved to hold the phial with refined fingers, and rub the liquid into the "raw" with the soft touch of love. The affected attenuation of voice and forced *retinu* of feeling, sometimes degenerating into a puppy's simper, bore such a contrast to the acerbity of the matter, that the effect, though often ludicrous, was increased tenfold. We may now read such a passage as we subjoin,[3] serving merely as a solitary example of the style; but it would be vain to try to estimate the effect from the mere allocation of vocables disjoined from the acrimony they collected in their passage through the ear and carried to the brain.

THE YOUNG AMATEURS

It would seem that conspiring circumstances at the time pointed to that kind of denouement which is the issue of an evil too great for society to bear. In Barclay's time, the increased demand for the physical material of the dissecting halls was supplied by a most convenient arrangement of places. There was the Infirmary a little to the west, where deaths were occurring several times a week, and many bodies left unclaimed by their friends. Then, at the back of Barclay's hall was a little "death's mailing" set apart for those who had been relieved of life in that refuge of the wretched, and, strangely enough, the windows looked out upon the tempting field; so that a man or woman, dreaming of no such fate, might die and be buried, and taken and dissected, all within the temporal space of a few days, and the physical of a few yards. No great wonder that there was there a rope-ladder of ominous intention, and a box with such accommodating appurtenances as would permit of the insertion of hooks at the end of lines, whereby it might be let down empty and light, and brought up full and heavy. Nor was it inappropriate that young Cullen, the grandson of *Celeberrimus*, should be the man who accomplished with greatest spirit these easy appropriations. Some will yet recollect how these young gouls grinned with a satanic pleasure, as they saw the heavy-looking sextons busy with the work which they were so soon to undo, if it was not also more than surmise that these grave men could smile in return, even while they were beating down the green sod, as if it were to remain till the greater resurrection, in place of the smaller.

As connected with the continued spoliation of this unfortunate little Golgotha, a story was current out of which was

formed a mock heroic imitation of the 17th book of the "Iliad."
It seemed that an old beggar of the name of Sandy M'Nab, who
used to be known in Edinburgh as a cripple ballad singer, had
died of almost pure old age in the Infirmary, and was, in due
time, consigned to that rest of which, as a peripatetic minstrel, he
had enjoyed so small a portion in this world. Yet how little one
knows of the fate to which he may be destined! Who could have
supposed that Sandy M'Nab, about whom nobody cared more
than to give him an occasional penny, and who was left to die in
an hospital, would become as famous, within a limited space, as
Patroclus. It seemed that Cullen and some others had, according
to their custom, appropriated the body of the minstrel, so far
as to have it safely deposited in the box, and that box carefully
placed below the window waiting for the application of the
rope, whereby it was to be drawn to the upper regions; but in
the meantime, some three or four of Monro's Trojans, jealous
of the Greeks, had got over the wall with the same intention
that had fired their opponents. Though the night was dark,
with only an occasional glimpse of a shy moon, who got herself
veiled every now and then, as if ashamed of those deeds of man
enacted under her light, the collegians soon ascertained that
their envied minstrel had been exhumed, yea, that that body,
which once contained a spirit all but cosmopolitan, was cribbed
and confined in Cullen's insatiable box. The discovery inflamed
an original intention of mere body-snatching into an emprise of
stratagetic war against their professional foes; and straightway
they commenced to remove the box to the other side of the yard,
with a view to getting it hoisted over the wall. But the work had
scarcely commenced, when the watchful enemy, who, in fact, all
the time were busily undoing the rope in the hall above, observed
the stratagem below; and issuing forth, some three or four
of them, under the influence of something more like chivalry
than the stealing of bodies, they commenced an attack upon
the intruders, which was met by a stout resistance. The box had
been removed to nearly the middle of the yard, and round the

sacred centre where lay the dead Patroclus, the battle raged with a fierceness not unworthy of the old and immortal conflict. At one time Sandy was in possession of the Barclayens, at another in that of the Monroites; so that the old quotation, which was subsequently incorporated in heroics, was perhaps never, in all time, so applicable,—*"Danai Trojanique cadaver manus commiserunt."* Taken and retaken, and guarded with menaces, the inner contest was, meanwhile, illustrated by hand-to-hand fights over the swelling tumuli, perhaps not less glorious in their small way than many which have involved the fate of a kingdom; and yet the object of the conflict was the body of a wandering beggar. Nor is it known how long this affray might have lasted, if some people in the neighbourhood, having heard the uproar, had not threatened, by getting to the top of the wall, to bring the champions before the authorities. The Monroites fled, and the object of all this contention was left in the hands of those who, by possession, had at least the prior right. The box was hoisted to the rooms amidst the acclamations of the conquerors. *"Sic hi alacres cadaver extulerunt e bello."*

The want of this fruitful field behoved afterwards, on the advent of Knox, to be supplied by increased exactions over the country; and hence came a more perfect organisation of a staff, composed of men who, without the excuse of a stimulus for science, were attracted to the work by the bribe of high payments. We have already seen to what extent that bribe reached; and whatever otherwise may be thought of those grim minions of the moon, they had more to stir the low passions of human nature than those older minions on the borders, who, for the sake of living steers, often made dead bodies. Science became the Nemesis of the dearest and most sacred affections; and what may appear strange enough, the students themselves engaged in the work with a feeling, as we have hinted, approaching to chivalry. They were sworn knights of the fair damsel Science, though the rites were those of Melpomene, with the grotesque shapes of those of Thalia. The midnight enterprises had charms for them, but they were death to those feelings of a Christian people, which require to be viewed as a natural and necessary part of a social fabric, to be tampered with only to the ruin of virtue. Among these knights at an earlier period stood Robert Liston, whose hardihood and coolness in such midnight adventures could only be equalled by his subsequent surgical handlings; and like all other vigorous and enthusiastic men, he had the power of enlisting associates, warmed by the fire he himself felt.

A favourite theatre for these dark deeds was the banks of the Forth, along which are to be seen many of those small unprotected graveyards which, attached to villages, are as the shadow of the life that is within them. Yes, grave or merry as the hamlet may be, that shadow is never awanting—often within the sound of the marriage-dance, and refusing to be illumined by the light of man's earthly happiness. Sometimes in poetics called the gnome that points to eternity, no man can but for a few brief moments of seducing joy keep his eye from the contemplation of it; and, whether he can or not, he must be content to lie within its dark outline. These are common thoughts, which are sometimes condemned as a species of moralising; yet surprise will not the less pass even into vertigo when we think of individuals of the same species reversing rites which even lower instincts shudder to touch. We are always looking for seriousness in nature, and it is long till we are forced to confess that she is continually mocking us.

> "*Usque adeo, res humanas vis abdita quædam*
> *Obterit et pulchros fasceis sævasque secureis*
> *Proculcare ac* LUDIBRIO SIBI HABERE *videtur.*"

On one occasion our anatomist, having got a companion up to the point of courage, resolved to pay a night-visit to one of these outlying places, where, from information he had gained, there had been deposited an object which had a charm to him other than that of the mere "thing." The man had died of a disease which the country practitioner had reported to Liston as something which had stimulated his curiosity, but which he could not be permitted by the friends to inquire into in the manner so much desired by doctors. The two knights got themselves arrayed as sailors—with the jacket, the sou'-wester, the unbraced trousers, striped shirt, and all the rest—and getting on board a pinnace, made their way to Cures. They had on arrival some time to pass before the coming of the eery hour when such work as they had on hand could be performed with the least chance of interruption. The night, as the principal performer described it, was as dark as the narrow house whereof they were to deprive the still inhabitant, so that even with the assistance of the doctor's apprentice, who went along with them, they had the greatest difficulty to discover the limited spot of their operations. But Liston had encountered such difficulties before, and then "what mattered if they should take the wrong one?" for with the exception of the pathological curiosity, as in this case, these children of science had no more scruples of choice. In a trice the game was bagged, as they sometimes described the work, and the boy, getting alarmed, flew off with the necessary injunction of secrecy, which only added to his alarm, as they could plainly perceive by the sounds of his rapid receding steps heard in the stillness of the haunted spot.

But the work there was generally the least difficult of such enterprises, for as yet the people had not throughout the rural districts been roused to the necessity of the night-watch, which afterwards became so common. The danger lay in the conveyance, which in this, as in most other instances, was by the means of a pair of strong shoulders. The burden was accordingly hoisted on Liston's broad back, and the two, stumbling over the green *tumuli*, got to the skirts, and away as far as they could from habitations. The field side of a thick hedge was the selected place of deposit until the morning gave them light for achieving the further migrations of the unconscious charge; and then there was to be sought out a place of rest for the two tars, wearied with travelling all day homewards in the north after so long a cruise in the South Sea. Nor was it long before a welcome light proclaimed to Liston, who knew the country, the small wayside inn, in which they would repose during the night. And there, to be sure, they got that easy entrance, if not jolly welcome, so often accorded to this good-hearted set of men. They were soon in harmony with the household, and especially with a "Mary the maid of the inn," who saw peculiar charms in seamen in general, and in our friend Robert in particular; nor was the admiration all on one side, though Mary's predilection for his kind was, as matters turned out, to be anything but auspicious to the concealed students. Then the coquetting was helped by a little warm drink, if not a song from the companion about a certain "sheer hulk," which lay somewhere else than behind the hedge.

All this, be it observed, had taken place by the kitchen fire— an appropriate place for benighted seamen; and it being now considerably beyond twelve, they were about to be shewn their room, when they were suddenly roused by a loud shout outside, the words, "Ship, ahoy!" being more distinctly heard by our *quasi* tars than they perhaps relished, for, after all, neither of our students, however they might impose upon Mary, felt very comfortable under the apprehension of being scanned by a true son of Neptune.

"That's my brother Bill," said the girl, as she ran to open the door; "I fear he has been drinking."

The door being opened, the "Ship, ahoy" entered; and what was the horror of Liston and his friend when they saw a round, good-humoured sailor staggering under the weight of that identical bag and its contents which they had placed behind the hedge only a very short time before!

"There," cried the blustering lad, who had clearly enough been drinking, as he threw the heavy load on the kitchen-floor with the something between a squash and thump which might have been expected from the nature of the contents—"there, and

29

if it aint something good, rot them chaps there who stole it."

"What is it?" said Mary.

"And why should I know? Ask them. Didn't they put the hulk behind a hedge when I was lying there trying to wear about upon t'other tack? What ho!" he continued, "where did you heave from? But first let's see what's the cargo."

And before the petrified students could bring up a sufficient energy to interfere, Bill's knife had severed the thick cord which bound the neck of the bag. Then mumbling to himself, "What under the hatches?" he exposed, by rolling down the mouth of the bag, the gray head of a man.

The tar's speech was choked in a moment, and while the girl uttered a loud scream, and rushed out into the darkness, there stood the brave seaman, whose courage was equal to an indifference in a hurricane of wind or war, with his mouth open, and his eyes fixed in his head, and his arms extended as if waiting for the swing of a rope; all which culminated in a shout of terror as he ran after his sister, and left the field to those who could not by their own arts or exertions have got the command of it. So true is it that man's extremity is also not only God's opportunity, but sometimes his own, though against His will and His laws. Not a moment was to be lost. Without binding again the bag, the burden was again upon the back of the now resolute Liston, and without having time to pay for their warm drink, or to remember Mary for her smiles, the adventurers were off on their way to the beach.

Of all the unfortunate places on the banks of the estuary resorted to for these midnight prowlings, no one was more remarkable than that romantic little death's croft, Rosyth, near to Limekilns. Close upon the seashore, from which it is divided by a rough dike, and with one or two melancholy-enough-looking trees at the back, it forms a prominent object of interest to the pleasure parties in the Forth; nor is it possible for even a very practical person to visit it, when the waves are dashing and brattling against the shore, to be unimpressed with the solitude and the stillness of the inhabitants, amidst the ceaseless sounds of what he might term nature's threnody sung over the achievements of the grim king. Often resorted to by strangers who love, because they require the stimulus of the poetry of external things, the more, perhaps, because they want the true well-spring of humanity within the heart, it is a favourite resort of the inhabitants of the village, where bereaved ones, chiefly lovers of course, sit and beguile their griefs by listening to these sounds, which they can easily fancy have been heard for so many generations, even by those who lie there, and who have themselves acted the same part. The few old gray head-stones, occasionally dashed by the surf, have their story, which is connected through centuries with the names of the villagers; and such melancholy musers find themselves more easily associated with a line of humble ancestors than can occur in the pedigrees of populous towns. Surely it is impossible that these holy feelings can have a final cause so indifferent to Him who, out of man's heart, however hardened, "brings the issues of love," that it can be overlooked, defeated, and mocked by that pride of science of which man makes an idol. The *ludibrium* referred to by Lucretius is in this instance, at least, of man's making; and if it is conceded to be necessary that the bodily system should be known, that necessity, which is so far of man's thought, must be restricted by that other necessity, which is altogether of God's.

It was not to be supposed that this romantic mailing should escape the observation of our anatomist. Nor did it; and we are specially reminded of the fact by an admission made by Liston himself, that, unpoetical and rough as he was, an incident once occurred here which touched him more than any operation he ever performed. On this occasion he and his friends had made use of a boat specially hired for the purpose—a mode of conveyance which subsequently passed into a custom, before the Limekilns people were roused from their apathy, and became next to frantic under circumstances which left it in doubt whether any one of them, husband, wife, father, mother, or lover, could say that their relations had not been stolen away from their cherished Rosyth. The adventurers studied their time so well that their boat would get alongside of the dike under the shade of night, and they could wile away an hour or two while they watched the opportunity of a descent. They were favoured by that inspissated moonlight, which was enough for their keen eyes, and not less keen hands, and yet might suffice to enable them to escape observation. But just as they were about to land they observed the figure of a young woman sitting near one of the head-stones. The stillness all about enabled them to hear deep sobs, as if the heart had been convulsed, and tried by these efforts to throw off the weight of a deep grief. The story was readable enough even by gouls, but so intent were they on their prey that they felt no response to these offerings of the stricken heart to Him who, for His own purposes, had struck it. The scene continued beyond the endurance of their patience, and science, as usual, murmured against Nature's decrees; but at length she who was thought an intruder rose, and after some movement of the arms, which came afterwards to be understood, slowly left the spot.

The coast, as the saying goes, was now at last clear, and with a bound the myrmidons overleaped the wall. They were presently on the spot where the female had been seated, and even in their hurry observed that the heart-broken creature had been occupied as her last act by throwing some silly bits of flowers over the grave,—signs which as little physically as morally interfered with their design of spoliation. In a few minutes the object they sought was in their possession, and if there was any care more than ordinary observed in putting all matters to right on the surface, it was the selfish wish to keep so convenient a place free from those suspicions which might bar another visit. Nay, so heartless were they, that one of the party, whether Liston himself we cannot say, though it would not have been unlike him, decorated his jacket by sticking one of the slips of offering into the button-hole. They now hurried with their burden to the boat and pushed off, but they had scarcely got beyond a few yards when they saw the same figure hurrying to the dike. The light of the moon was now brighter, and they could easily observe the figure as it passed hurriedly, as if in great excitement, backwards and forwards, occasionally holding out the arms, and uttering the most melancholy sounds that ever came from the human heart. It might be that as yet she had hope in mere adjuration, but as the boat moved further and further away, there came a shrill wail, so piercing that it might have been heard even at the distance of the village. But heedless of an appeal, which nature responded to faithfully by an echo, they rowed away, still hearing, in spite of the splash of the oars, the same wail as it gradually became faint in their increasing distance. At length they could hear nothing but the sweltering of the waters, and Rosyth with its solitary mourner bade fair to be forgotten under the Lethe of the flask, which on such occasions was never awanting.

This story was very soon made readable to Liston and the others by the concatenation of certain very simple circumstances. A newspaper report which Liston had seen some days before, had announced the death, by drowning, of a young sailor belonging to Limekilns. The account was sufficiently lugubrious for any readers; but the editor, as usual, had mixed up with it, whether truly or not, the old story of love and impending marriage; the object too being, of course, young, brave, virtuous, and comely. Then came the account of the funeral, also touchingly given. But it seemed that all this poetry had been thrown away upon the ardent anatomist; nor even when afterwards, in the hall, he became satisfied that he had secured the right object, would he in his heart admit that he had in this adventure done anything more than would be justified by the use he could make of his knowledge in ameliorating physical evils in his fellow-men, however dearly that advantage might have been acquired in the agony of that figure he had left wailing at Rosyth. Yet it is but fair to say that Liston himself admitted that the sound of that cry, the sight of those wringing hands, and the rapid goings to and fro of the shade on the shore, never passed from his memory.

Robert Liston, beyond all the others, carried so much of the spirit of chivalry into his adventures of body-snatching, that he thought it as noble an act to carry off a corpse as an ancient knight-errant did to bear off a prisoner; but his followers were more like mimallons than myrmidons, and required more of the flask to keep up their spirits. Some of these youths once made a mistake at Rosyth. Having run up their boat, they proceeded to the little death's croft to take up the body of a woman who had died in child-bed. The night was dark and gusty, and the wind whistled through the long grass as if Nænia had been presiding there to hear her own doleful music; but our youths cared little for these things, and, after twenty minutes' work, they pulled up "the tall beauty," as they called her after they got home. Away they hurried her to the dike, upon which they laid her, till two got over to place her in the boat. All seemed fair, but just at the moment, some ill-mannered tyke set up, without the excuse of a moon,—for she was far enough away beyond the shadows,—a deep howl, so prolonged and mournful, that even all the potency of the flask could not save them from being struck with awe, as well as a fear of detection. But they had more to be afraid of, for almost immediately after, one of them called out, "There's a lantern among the graves;" and thus flurried, yet determined not to lose their prize, they rugged the body from the top of the rubble dike so roughly, if not violently, that a great portion of the long hair, which had got entangled among the stones, was, along with a piece of the scalp, torn away, and left hanging on the other side. Safe on board, they lost no time in pushing off, in spite of the surly breakers that threatened to detain them; nor did they now care for either the dog or the lantern, the latter of which they saw through the dark medium, dodging towards the very spot they had left, and then remain stationary there, as if the bearer had been stayed and petrified by the relic they had left. Up to not a very late period, the story went in the neighbourhood that he who bore the lantern was the husband of "the tall beauty," and that he discovered the hair, and knew from the colour, which nearly approached flaxen, that it was that of his wife, whose untimely death had rendered him frantic.

There was no loss in that case; but another which was current among the classes not long after was less fortunate, though not less true, as indeed may be verified by the brother, still living, of the young student who figured in it. Somewhere about Gilmerton or Liberton, we are uncertain which, a small farmer who had lost his wife went out one morning very early, probably because he could not rest in his bed for the dreary blank that was there,—that negative so much more appalling to love than the dead positive. On going along the Edinburgh road, he observed some white figure lying close by the footpath, and making up to see what it was, he came upon the corpse of a woman, dressed in her scolloped dead-clothes, and lying extended upon her back, with the "starr eyes" open, glazed, and fixed. On looking more narrowly, he discovered that it was his own wife, and, all dismayed and wild as he became, he could still have the power to think that she had come back to life after having been buried and lain in the grave for three days, and had thus far struggled to get to her beloved home. Frenzy knows nothing of logic, and was he to think how she could have thrown off a ton of earth and got up again to the light of the sun? The idea took him by force, and, throwing himself upon the body, he looked into the dead orbs, and watched the cold stiff lips, and listened for a breath. Vain heart, with all its hopes and tumults! no sign in return for all this madness. Yet he persevered, and gave up, and resumed, and, as the hope died to come back again, he writhed his strong body in an agony tenfold more acute than his first grief; nor would he in all probability have renounced the insane hope for a much longer time, if the Penicuik carrier had not come up, and, hearing the wonderful tale, hinted the explanation of an interrupted body-snatching. The light flashed upon him in an instant, and, in pursuance of a desire to keep the occurrence secret for the sake of her friends, he prevailed upon the man to take the body in the cart and remove it to his house. It was buried again privately on the following night, and few ever heard of the occurrence. And now comes the explanation of a story which may seem altogether incredible. A young student of the name of F——y, belonging to Monro's class, entered with two others into an adventure of body-snatching, in imitation of those whose exploits had produced in them an enthusiasm untempered by prudence, and not directed by experience. They fixed upon their ground, and hired a gig, and the hour was regulated by an obituary. Away accordingly they set, with no more knowledge of the secrets of the art than what they could get from the regular purveyors of the class, but provided with the necessary instrument. They soon got to their destination, and, leaving the gig in the charge of one of them, the two others got over the low wall, and, by the aid of the moon, discovered the last laid turf. Going to work vigorously, they succeeded in raising the body of a woman, but not having brought from the gig the indispensable sack, and, being fluttered and hurried, they bethought themselves of carrying the object to the side of the road, just as it was with the dead-clothes, and then running along by the side of the hedge to where their companion waited. F——y accordingly, with the aid of his friend, got the white burden hoisted on his back, holding it as firmly as he could by the linen. So far all was well, and they were fortunate, moreover, in getting out by a gate which they could open; but just as F——y got to the road, along which he had to go a considerable space, the grasp he had of the shroud began to give way, perhaps almost unknown to himself, the effect of which was that the body slipped so far down that the feet touched the ground. The consequence was altogether peculiar; as F——y bent and dodged in the hurry of getting forward, the feet of the corpse, coming always to the ground, resiled again with something like elasticity, so that it appeared to him as if it trotted or leaped behind him. Fear is the mother of suspicion, and the idea took hold of him that the body was alive. He uttered a roar,—threw his burden off, and crying out to his friend, "By G——, she's alive!" jumped into the gig. His friend was taken by the same terror, and away they galloped, leaving the corpse in the place where it was found next morning by the husband.

THE REGULAR STAFF

It is, we think, laid down in that strange book of Robert Forsyth's on morals, that the gratification of the desire of knowledge is, at least on this earth of ours, the true end of man; and, no doubt, were we to judge of the strength of this desire in forcing man down into the bowels of the earth, and up into the heavens, across unknown seas, and over equally unknown continents, we would not be slow to confess its great power. And yet how many there are who assign the same place to the power of mammon, while others stand up for love and the social affections! We will not presume to decide where the range goes from the things of earth to those of heaven; but it appears pretty certain that there have been a good many Charles Kirkpatrick Sharpes, who have lauded, while in health, the practice of leaving the body to the doctors, and who yet have shrunk from the personal example when the shadow of the dark angel was over them. There have been also, we suspect, fewer Jeremy Benthams, who actually have left their carrion to the vultures of science, than of Merryleeses, who have robbed churchyards, and sold the stolen article for money.[4] Nor, in estimating the motives of the few scientific testators, can we say that we have much belief in their professions, if it is not more true that they are only seekers of notoriety, sometimes, as in the case of the author of the Fallacies, so weak as to be bribed by the offer of having their skins tanned and distributed in slips—the skin being, in such instances, the most valuable part of their corporations.

In pursuance of these notions, we may safely infer that if the wants of the halls had been left to be supplied by the scientific zeal of the amateurs, the state of anatomy would have been less perfect than we find it under the auspices of such men as

Schwann, or Bell, or Hall, in our day. And we say this without being much satisfied that all the boasted discoveries have led to much more than the conviction that we get deeper and deeper into the dark, while—admitting many ameliorations—the people recover from operations, or die of diseases, very much as they used to do. What are called the high cases might very well be left alone, so that we might be still bound to admit that Nature's purpose, in imposing the sacred feeling for the dead, is consistent with her determination, that if in this defeated by man, he shall earn nothing by trying to get at her secrets. But there was no necessity that the matter of purveyance should be left to the students. There have always been body-thieves; but the time had come in Scotland, when not only their number behoved to be increased, but their energies also, by the multiplied demands of the halls.

How far this increase might have progressed, but for the great drama of "The Scotch Court of Cacus," it is impossible to say; but for a time the staff of Knox's artists were rather put upon their wits and exertions, than increased by dangerous bunglers. The trade was perilous, and required attributes not very often found united,—a total bluntness of feeling, a certain amount of low courage, much ingenuity of device, clever personal handling, and total disregard of public opinion—the love of money being the governing stimulant. Few classes of men could have afforded a better study in the lower and grosser parts of human nature. There was one called Merrylees, or more often Merry-Andrew, a great favourite with the students. Of gigantic height, he was thin and gaunt, even to ridiculousness, with a long pale face, and the jaws of an ogre. His shabby clothes, no doubt made for some tall person of proportionate girth, hung upon his sharp joints, more as if they had been placed there to dry than to clothe and keep warm. Nor less grotesque were the motions and gestures of this strange being. It seemed as if he went upon springs, and even the muscles of his face, as they passed from the grin of idiot pleasure to the scowl of anger, seemed to obey a similar power. Every movement was a spasm, as if the long lank muscles, unable to effect a contraction through such a length, accomplished their object by the concentrated energy of violent snatches. So, too, with the moral part: the normal but grotesque gravity was only to be disturbed by some sudden access of passion, which made him toss his arms and gesticulate. So completely was he the cause of fun in others, that often on the street some larking student would cry out, "Merry-Andrew," for no other purpose than to see him wheel about, clench his hands, and throw his face into all manner of furious contortions. All this only conspired to make him a butt, and the loud laugh which always came when there was nothing to laugh at, or rather something which would have produced gravity in another, helped the consummation.

Yet withal this same idiot was the king of Knox's artists. Nothing dared him, and nothing shamed him, if he was not even proud of a profession which was patronised by gentlemen and men of science, and paid at a rate which might have put industrious and honest tradesmen to the blush. Like many other half simpletons, too, he had a fertility of device in attaining his object, which insured success, when others apparently more intelligent despaired. So he was a leader upon whom often depended the hopes of the students, when their material was scarce or awanting. When not engaged in his rural exploits, he was always hanging about the Infirmary, where, no doubt, he was in secret communication with the *élèves* of that institution connected with Knox's rooms. From these he got intelligence of likely deaths, where there was a chance of the persons not being soon claimed by their relatives. Now was the opportunity of this genius. He kept a brown black suit for the occasion of a mourner, repaired to the Infirmary, and acted the part of the relative to such perfection, that the nurses at least—for the medical men could wink—were deceived. Nay, he looked at all times so much the afflicted, that the personation even to something like tears was as easy to him as to the weeper in the House of Commons, who cried "like a crocodile with his hands in his breeches' pockets." The moment the body was got outside in the white coffin, the bearers actually *ran* with it to the hall, under the inspiration of the, to such glandered hacks in the shape of men, so enormous a reward.

Another of the leaders, though far inferior to Merrylees, was the "Spune," a name given to a man whose real one was scarcely known in the rooms, and which was supposed to indicate some superior genius in lifting out the contents of a coffin. He was a littleish man, with a clean-shaved face, surmounting a dirty black suit, worn down to the cotton, which time had glazed. One would have taken him not certainly for a remunerated Methodist preacher, but one who would have given a great amount of doctrine for as much as would have got him a dinner. Yet he was in reality a mute, being one of those dumb worshippers of philosophy whose thoughts, going down into the earth, if not up to heaven, are too deep and sacred for human speech. Nay, so grave, precise, and wise did he look, that you would have said he bore all the honours of the science to the advancement of which he contributed so much; nor is it certain that he did not really feel—so necessary if not indispensable they considered themselves to be to the professors—that he was engaged in the holy cause of the advancement of mankind and the amelioration of their natural ills,—a conviction this, on the part of the "Spune," not modified by the reception of his fee, which he considered to be the wages of virtue; for while Merry-Andrew clutched his reward with a spasm and a spring, his compeer took his with the dignity and nonchalance of one who laboured for the benefit of his species. However ludicrous all this, one could scarcely say that it was out of place, for without the "Spune" the indagators in the hall would have had small chance of extracting anything from that deep well where it is said truth can alone be found.

Another was a man whose real name was Mowatt, but who was christened by the professional appellation of "Moudewart," (*moldewarp,*) sufficiently indicative of his calling in burrowing into the bowels of the earth. An old plasterer, too lazy to work, he had betaken himself to this trade from a mere love of the money, so that he behoved to rank in a much lower grade than the "Spune." Then, so essentially insensible was he to the honour of contributing to science, that he did not take on a particle of dignity, even from the sympathy of his fellow-labourers. It might be in vain that the "Spune" tried to impress him with the importance of his calling,—he was a man of merely so many pounds for what is in the bag, and no more. Without that principle of receptivity which enables a congenial soul to take on the reflection of the beauty or honour of an act, he was equally dead to the sublime inspiration of knowledge. Even Merry-Andrew had collected some scientific terms—such as *caput*, or *cranium*, sometimes even attempting *occiput*—all parts of the body with which alone he had anything to do in the process of abstraction; and as for the "Spune," he could even discourse of *tibias* and *fibulas*, if he did not stagger under *os coccygis*, in a manner which might have made his companion prick up his ear at the wonder that any such head could carry such terms. But what can be done with a man who has no symptoms of a human soul but that which shews itself when the eye counts with something like pleasure the price of a human body? Yet, strange enough, and perhaps unjustly enough, the two others were not more prized by their patrons than this degraded son of science, who served their purpose equally well—a fact which would have brought down the learned dignity of his co-labourers if they had had sense enough to notice it.

The others of the staff (the names of some of whom we could give) were not to be compared to these leaders—not even to the "Moudiewart," who, however stupid in respect to the science, was really sufficiently up to "the thing" to entitle him to rank as a successful if not respectable merchant. They were so utterly insensate, that they could not even commit the great mistake of supposing that their occupation degraded them, for the good reason that they were unconscious of degradation. Not that they were unhappy in consequence of not liking the work, for they were even fond of it as a means of getting them drink and tobacco, without the hope of which they might have been dull or sad, but not unhappy, a term which implies something like intelligence, if not sentiment. Fitted only for the humblest parts of the calling—the carrying, the watching, the calling out when intruders loomed in the distance—they had no envy towards the higher orders, and being thus free from all care, they could sing or whistle beneath the burden of a poet without thinking that they desecrated the profession of the Muses. We might thus liken them to those interlusive gentry who play the punning parts of a terribly deep tragedy, and who, not knowing where the pathos lies, as when Hamlet discourses on the skull, are contented with the duty of shovelling out either soil or song.

If we were inclined to moralise a little on the condition of such men as these, if men they can be called, we would hesitate to subscribe to the old Johnsonian notion that happiness has any relation to the number of ideas that pass through the mind, if we would not go to the other extreme, that for aught we know, there may be as much of that kind of thing between the shells of an oyster as between the ribs of a human being—at least the question must remain unsettled until we come again in the round of changes to the doctrine of transmigration of souls. The world is full of the examples of the meeting of extremes; and if you want one more, just take that afforded by the fact that these men we have been describing could carry on their shoulders in a canvas bag a Rothschild or a Byron, and never think that they were to any degree honoured by the burden. All one to them— the beautiful young creature who died of a scorned affection, the shrivelled miser who expired in a clutch of his gold, or the old gaberlunzie whose puckered lungs could no longer inflate themselves or the bagpipes which once received so joyfully the superabundant wind. But seriously, although these things have been, are we entitled to go with the fatalist, who says that what is, is as it ought to be? Though the wily fox contrived to get his neighbours to cut off their tails to make them like himself in his misfortune of being excaudated, is that any reason why nature should repeal her law and produce therefore tailless foxes? We hope not. And so also, because science run mad decreed that she should be served by such men and such acts, in opposition to the first and last throbbings of the love of kindred, is that any reason why nature should renounce her right of forming man in the image of God, and with affections which are to endure through all eternity? But we have even now, when it is whispered that subjects are again becoming scarce, men of the Christian faith who speak lightly of the dead human frame as nothing when deprived of the spirit. This may do for the logic of physics, but we have been led to believe that the religion we profess is not that of Merry-Andrew or the "Spune," but a divine intimation that the temple of the soul is not limited to the time of the earth—yea, that it is something which, *only changed*, shall rise again and endure for ever. Even this is not adverse to the claims of science; but as a shade distinguishes homicide and murder, so does a shade distinguish between science in reverence to God, and science in desecration of His first and most universal laws.

SYMPATHISING SEXTONS, DOCTORS, AND RELATIVES

All forces are measured by opposition, as, indeed, all the phenomena of nature are known to us by comparison, and so, in all fairness, we must estimate the turpitude of the professors and students the more lightly, in proportion to their freedom from all endearing feelings of recognition or friendship towards those whose remains came within their studies. The same metre is due to the class of purveyors, and Heaven knows how much, after all this abatement, remained at their debit, cognisant as they behoved to be of the certainty that they were sowing the bitter seeds of misery throughout the land. But what are we to say of others—doctors in the country who were privy to the remunerated exhumation of their patients—sextons who gave the pregnant hint, and then went to sleep in the expectation of a fee in the morning—nay, of those, and such at that time were counted among human beings, who bartered their friends and relatives for a smile of mammon?

Out of these materials how easy could it be to add so much, and so many more darker shades to the picture. We have no great wish to lay them on either thick or thin—the mind will paint for itself, as rises the contemplation: the family doctor hanging over his patient with professional sympathy, and perhaps something finer, dreaming the while of a *post-obit* fee, in addition to that paid for his skill to cure—the sexton clapping down the sod over a companion who had often set the table in a roar, in which the grave official had joined, and meditating a resurrection through his means in the morning—the relative who had even got the length of tears, dropping them on the pale face of an old friend, all the while that he meditated a sale of the body. But it is true that the annals of the period justified all these grim pictures. Many will still recollect the young Irish doctor who went in the Square under the name of the "Captain"—a man of such infinite spirits, always in a flow of his country's humour, that you could not suppose that there was time or room in his mind for a little smooth pool to reflect a passing cloud of sadness. In his native town he drove a great trade for the Edinburgh halls—his largest contribution being laid on the graveyard of his native town. And surely, in his case, we would have thought the Chinese system of paying a doctor, only in the case of recovery, would have been an example of Irish prudence. Nay, so many were the barrels, with a peculiar species of *contenu*, he sent by Leith, that it was difficult to avoid the suspicion that the rollicking son of Erin had a faith in his medicines stronger than the hope which illumined the faces of his patients. These barrels of the "Captain" were quite well known, not only to the skippers, but the porters about the pier, ay, even the carters who made the final transport; and here, again, mammon was the seducing spirit. It was only when he came over for his large accumulated payments that he was seen in the hall, where his jokes and immeasurable laughter might have made those quiet heads on the tables rise to get a look of their once sympathising surgeon. Nor, in the consideration of the students, was his laughter unjustified by his jokes; as once where, pointing to a certain table, he apostrophised the burden it carried—"Ah, Misthress O'Neil! did I spare the whisky on you, which you loved so well,—and didn't you lave me a purty little sum to keep the resurrectionists away from you,—and didn't I take care of you myself? and by J——s you are there, and don't thank me for coming over to see you;" or when, in the same brogue, he told them that, not long before his coming over, he had, for lack of "the thing" in his own town, taken a car and rode to a neighbouring village, where he got precisely what he wanted; that, on returning at a rapid rate with his charge, he met the mother of it with the words in her mouth—

"Well, docther, is it all right wid the grave ov poor Pat?"

"All right, misthress. Didn't I tell you afore there were no resurrectionists in that quarter?"

"And you are sure you eximined it complately?"

"No doubt in the wide earth."

"Then I may go back, and you'll give me a ride?"

"Surely, and plaisant," said he; "just get up."

"And," continued the Captain to the delighted students, "I dhrove the good lady home agin without breaking a bone of her body, and Pat never said a word."

"But," he went on, "if I were to tell you all my Irish work, I would never get back to my ould country agin."

"Just another adventure, Captain."

"Well, then, didn't a purty young girl—and I have hopes of her yet for myself, for she has money galore—come to me one day in a mighty fit of grief?"

"'My poor mother has been rizzt,' said she, as she burst out in the way of these gentle craturs.

"'And she has not,' said I—(the more by token that I had the ould lady in the house.)

"'I have been at the grave,' said she, 'and I see it has been disturbed.'

"'And it has not,' said I; 'for wasn't I there this morning before ever a soul in all the town was stirring? and didn't I leave it all right with my ould friend?'

"'But I have seen marks,' said she again; for she was so determined.

"'And do you think I don't know you have?' said I; 'and didn't I see them, after I got a spade from the sexton and put on a nate sod or two more to make the grave dacent and respectable?'

"'Oh, I'm so glad,' replied she, all of a content.

"'And you'll be gladder yet, my darling,' said I, as I gave her a kiss. 'Go home and contint yourself, and perhaps, when your mournings are off, you may consent to make a poor docther happy.'

"And so she went away, blushing as no one ever saw except in a raal rose."

And the laugh again sounded through the hall among the dead.

Whether these stories were true, or merely got up by the extravagant love of fun in the Captain, it would not be easy to say; but certain it is, that their being told and responded to in the manner thus described, from the lips of an ear-witness, shews us the atmosphere of moral feeling that then obtained in places proudly designated as being dedicated to the interests of humanity, and from which, too, we could draw the conclusion that what was gained in the amelioration of physical disease was required to be debited so largely with the deterioration of morals and a wide-spread infliction of pain. But even darker deeds were done in Scotland than those for which the Captain took so gasconading a credit. From a certain village called S——e, the myrmidons of the Square, and particularly the "Spune," got more material for the Hall than could have been expected without a resident sympathiser and participator in the profits. That zealous correspondent was not the sexton—no, nor the minister; but he was the minister's brother, and, so far as we can learn, a member of the profession. Need it be remarked how convenient the relation between the messenger of heaven and the benefactor of earth—the physician of souls and the curer of bodies—the man of prayers and the man of pills—the distributor of the great catholicon and the dispenser of the small! We can fancy the godly man, we believe all unconscious of the intentions of his brother, pouring the holy unction of his prayers over the struggling spirit of the dying Christian, and the doctor counting the pulses as they died away into that stillness which was to be the prelude to the payment—five pounds—for the deserted temple. One recording angel would fly to heaven with a name to be inscribed in the roll of eternal salvation, and the other to Edinburgh to announce that another body was to be inserted in the black list of Surgeon's Square.

Even this was not the culmination of the evil. The head of the scorpion—society—was to swallow its tail, so that the virtue and the poison would meet and traverse together the circle. Mammon, through the medium of the leaders of the purveyors of science, extended his charm to the hearts of relations and friends, changing the soft glance of love and pity into the fiery glare of sordid rapacity. Throughout the High Street and Canongate, and down through the squalid wynds and closes, where, though crime and misery shake hands over the bottle of whisky, the death-bed still retains some claims over the affections, and where religion is sometimes able to extort from the demons of passion the unwilling tribute of compunction, these strange men prowled in the hope of finding or making a monster. And in this it is certain that they succeeded more often than was then suspected, or is even yet known. Their first inquiry was for death-beds, and the next for evidence of squalid poverty combined with vice. The subject was approached cautiously where the ground had all the appearance of being dangerous. If they were met by deliberation or hesitation, between which and blows there was no space, their object was secured, as the devil's is, by exposing to the haggard eye of penury the very form and substance of the bribe. In one case, reported by Merrylees himself, the bargain was struck in a whisper by the bed-side of the dying friend. How far the relationship extended in any of these cases we never could ascertain; and it is only fair to assume, for the sake of human nature, that in the majority of instances the success was only over the keepers of stray lodgers, and mere friends, as distinguished from relatives; but that there were, some where there behoved to be the yearnings of affection, and a consequent struggle between love and mammon, there can be no doubt.

Thus, however difficult or delicate the moral impediments that required to be overcome, the physical parts of the contract were of easy management. The coffining was made a little ceremony, performed in presence of some of the neighbours. There would be tears, no doubt, if not an Irish howl, and the louder perhaps the greater the bribe; and in the evening a bag of tanners' bark supplied the place of the friend of the many virtues discoursed of at the wake. Nor was there less care taken in carrying this box of bark to the Canongate burying-ground than was displayed by "Merry-Andrew" in conveying the *surrogatum* to Surgeon's Square; but, of course, there would be a difference in the speed of the respective bearers. Taking all these details into account, we can scarcely deny that these men wrought harder for their money than if they had pursued a regular calling. But, then, they liked it. Even after the bargain for the living invalid was struck, how many anxious watchings at a wynd-end were to exhaust the weary hours before the spirit took wing from the sold body! The gaunt figure of Merrylees, as he jerked his lank muscles and threw his face into the old contortions, might be seen there, but none would know what this meant.

One night, a student who saw him standing at a close-end, and suspected that his friend was watching his prey, whispered in his ear, "She's dead," and, aided by the darkness, escaped. In a moment after, "Merry-Andrew" shot down the wynd, and, opening the door, pushed his lugubrious face into a house.

"It's a' owre I hear," said he, in a loud whisper; "and when will we come for the body?"

"Whisht, ye mongrel," replied the old harridan who acted as nurse; "she's as lively as a cricket."

A statement which, though whispered in the unction of secrecy, and with most evident sincerity, Merrylees doubted, under a suspicion that the woman's conscience had come between her and the love of money; and, jerking himself forward to the bed, he threw the shadow of his revolting countenance over the face of the terrified invalid, enough of itself to have sent the hovering spirit to its destination, whether above or below. Not a word was spoken by the victim. She had heard enough to rouse terror sufficient to deprive her of speech, if not of breath; and all that the ogre witnessed was the pair of eyes lighted up with the parting rays of the fluttering spirit, and peering mysteriously as if into his very soul.

But then, as it happened, "Merry-Andrew" had only a body, and this look, more like as it was to a phosphoric gleam than the light of the living spirit, fell blank. Enough for him that she was not yet dead; and, taking one of his springing steps, he was out of the room, forcing his way up the wynd, to seek, and, if possible, to wreak a most imprudent vengeance on the larking prig who had put his long muscles to such unfruitful exercise. Meanwhile, the young rogue had waited for the butt, to see some more of his picturesque spasms; nor was he disappointed, for the moment Merrylees cast his eye on him, he tossed up his hands, and, with a shout which might have been taken by one who did not know him, or even by one who did, as an indication either of intense fun or fiery anger, made after him at the rate of his long strides. The student, of course, escaped, and Merrylees, convinced that the invalid was not so near her end as he wished, went growling home to bed.

But this tragedy, with its ephialtic forms reflecting these coruscations of grim comedy, did not end here. The old invalid, no doubt hastened by what she had witnessed, died on the following night; and on that after the next succeeding, when he had reason to expect that she would be conveniently placed in that white fir receptacle that has a shape so peculiarly its own, and not deemed by him so artistic as that of a bag or a box, Merrylees, accompanied by the "Spune," entered the dead room with the sackful of bark. To their astonishment, and what Merrylees even called disgusting to an honourable mind, the old wretch had scruples.

"A light has come doon upon me frae heaven," she said, "and I canna."

"Light frae heaven!" said Merrylees indignantly. "Will that shew the doctors how to cut a cancer out o' ye, ye auld fule? But we'll sune put out that light," he whispered to his companion. "Awa' and bring in a half-mutchkin."

"Ay," replied the "Spune," as he got hold of a bottle, "we are only obeying the will o' God. 'Man's infirmities shall verily be cured by the light o' His wisdom.' I forget the text."

And the "Spune," proud of his biblical learning, went upon his mission. He was back in a few minutes; for where in Scotland is whisky not easily got?

Then Merrylees, (as he used to tell the story to some of the students, to which we cannot be expected to be strictly true as regards every act or word,) filling out a glass, handed it to the wavering witch.

"Tak' ye that," he said, "and it will drive the deevil out o' ye."

And finding that she easily complied, he filled out another, which went in the same direction with no less relish.

"And noo," said he, as he saw her scruples melting in the liquid fire, and took out a pound-note, which he held between her face and the candle, "look through that, ye auld deevil, and ye'll see some o' the real light o' heaven that will mak' your cats' een reel."

"But that's only ane," said the now-wavering merchant, "and ye ken ye promised three."

"And here they are," replied he, as he held before her the money to the amount of which she had only had an experience in her dreams, and which reduced her staggering reason to a vestige.

"Weel," she at length said, "ye may tak' her."

And all things thus bade fair for the completion of the barter, when the men, and scarcely less the woman, were startled by a knock at the door, which having been opened, to the dismay of the purchasers there entered a person, dressed in a loose great-coat, with a broad bonnet on his head, and a thick cravat round his throat, so broad as to conceal a part of his face.

"Mrs Wilson is dead?" said the stranger, as he approached the bed.

"Ay," replied the woman, from whom even the whisky could not keep off an ague of fear.

"I am her nephew," continued the stranger, "and I am come to pay the last duties of affection to one who was kind to me when I was a boy. Can I see her?"

"Ay," said the woman; "she's no screwed doon yet."

Enough for "Merry-Andrew" and the "Spune." They were off, and up the wynd in a moment, followed by the stranger, who, for some reason that has not in the story yet appeared, gave them chase, only so much as to terrify them into a flight, but without being carried so far as to insure a seizure, which he did not seem inclined to achieve. Nor did he return to bury Mrs Wilson—a strange mystery to the unnatural nurse, who, however, did not lose all, for the three pounds had been left on the table, and were quickly appropriated without the least consideration.

The story next day went the round of the hall; and it was not until the woman was buried, that Merrylees and his friend were made aware that the same student who had played the principal performer at the head of the wynd was the stranger in a very well-assorted disguise.

PREYING
ON EACH OTHER

We are surprised when we find a man turn wicked all of a sudden, and seldom think that we are simply drawing a false conclusion, insomuch as the suddenness of the supposed change is a mere jump of development,—the consequence of a long train, dating perhaps from infancy. So true is it, that the increase of depravity is the progression of degrees, all according to that law of nature whereby God wills to act by the regular process of cause and effect, each change helping another, till matters come to a burst, when the often-split powers take new directions, to begin in new courses, and go on increasing as before. We have already seen the demon mammon obeying the law of increased power, spreading from a centre in Surgeon's Square among the people, and trying heart after heart, even to that core where he battled successfully with affections which God seems to have consecrated to Himself. Yes; and the demon was to go farther and farther,—even beyond the stage where we are sure to find him,—contesting even the breasts of the regular traders, the very centres of their natural affinities.

We have already noticed the use to which "Merry-Andrew" put that brown-black suit of his, the white neckcloth, the haggard cheeks, and the tears,—all so often the stage property in the melodrama of life, and as easily put off as the personation of the character, unless kept on by the adhesive effect of a good legacy. But as every man is once or twice in his life doomed to experience in reality that which he falsifies in theory, so our mourner over those he had never seen before was on one occasion, at least, placed in a position where it might have been

54

expected he would experience something like a qualm about the thing which was in form, if not in consistency, a heart. It seems that Merrylees had a sister in Penicuik, with whom he had been brought up, and towards whom, before he had experienced the hardening process of mammon's manipulations, he had entertained something like affection. That sister happened to die; and, on a certain day, Merrylees appeared in the Square once more in the old suit which had so faithfully repaid its original cost twenty times over. He had sense enough—and the reason thereof may appear, on a little consideration of the character of his compeers—to keep the circumstance of the death to himself; and, accordingly, when the apparition appeared in the ominous suit, they anticipated another descent of grief upon the Infirmary.

This suspicion very soon passed away, for not only was there no sign of that puckering up of the lank muscles, not deserving the name of a look of vivacity, which preceded his lugubrious personation in the hospital, but the day passed without any aid being asked from the others to help to carry, or rather run, with the white coffin. The methodist "Spune" was the first to divine the real cause of the chief's melancholy; and whether it was, as was said,—for we are not certain of the fact,—that the two had had a quarrel some time before about the division of spoil, it was certain that the worsted competitor began to entertain some very dark thoughts about a visit to Penicuik church-yard, whereby he could not only remunerate himself in the shape of money, but achieve one of the most curious revenges that ever were enjoyed since Nemesis began to have her fiery eyes. So, taking Mowat to a side of the Square, the "Spune" began to look mysteriously into his face—a most unnecessary process, where there never was any change of expression since first nature squeezed the clay into solidity.

"I suspect Merrylees' sister's dead at last," said he; "isn't she as good as another?"

"Nae difference," was the answer, without any surprise.

"Yes, ye fule, some; and you're so stupid you don't see it."

"I can see nane,—a' is alike to me; ae worm's as gude's anither to the 'Moudiewart.'"

"Ay, but if a worm had bitten ye, man, wouldn't you squeeze it the harder?"

"Maybe."

"And have you forgotten the ten shillings in Blackfriars' Wynd?"

"I'll tak it oot o' his blude," was the surly reply.

"And why not out of his sister's?" said the "Spune," with another dark look as unnecessary as the former.

"Just as sune,—a' ane."

"And," continued the tempter, where no temptation was necessary, "I know where she lies, just in the southeast angle, where he told me his father was laid."

"Why no him?" replied Mowat; "a' ane."

"Rotten ten years ago, you idiot," said the other, getting impatient.

"Weel, the fresh ane then."

"Now you are sensible," continued the friendly counsellor; "we might have her here in the morning, with five pounds each in our pockets, and a laugh in our sleeves at Merrylees."

"I never saw you laugh," said Mowat, in perfect innocence.

"No more you did, nor any other person, 'cause its always in the sleeve. Doesn't do to laugh about these things—they're scientific."

"Umph! dinna understand that; but I'm ready when you like."

"That's right," replied the gratified "Spune." "Have Cameron's donkey and cart at the south end of Newington by ten o'clock. It's moonlight, I think."

"Dinna ken, but it's a' ane. I'll be there; but, mind, you stand the whisky this time."

And so (having indulged, perhaps, in our own way of putting this conversation—the *contenu* being the same) the important enterprise was arranged with that zest on the part of the grave and precise principal which results from secrecy; for it was impossible to suppose that Merrylees could suspect that even they were capable of preying on their fellow-labourer, and robbing the nest of any affections that might hang about it.

At the appointed time the "Moudiewart" was at his post with the little cuddy and the cart, where he was soon joined by his friend. Away they went,—Mowat driving, and the "Spune" lying extended in the vehicle, in utter disregard of the poor animal, not much larger than himself. With such an object before them, comprehending within the success of its acquisition the gratification of two of the strongest passions of degraded man, and no sensibility to admit of the feeling of a reaction in the quietness of the road and the increasing stillness of the hour, with, in addition, an auspicious moon, in whose face they could look only as a light-giving thing that makes gnomes out of head-stones, they might have been supposed to be merry. But no, there were no salient points in their natures from which could spring even that mirth which rides on the back of horrors. Mutely they drove along, with no sounds to break the silence, save the patter of the donkey's feet and the turns of the wheels. Very different this silent progress from those expeditions in which Merrylees formed a part, and where, if there was necessarily absent everything like the rational discourse of human beings, there was yet something to relieve the monotony in the shout after draining off a glass, the muscular contortions, and the *bizarres étourderies* of their strange friend. It was the caravan without the fool, and even he, as a son of Momus and Angerona, or some such mongrels, was a droll against his will. Sad fate to him who, even in his efforts not to be the cause of mirth in others, could himself become the butt of those whom, not more stupid, he could, in his self-protection, afford to despise. But Merrylees had at length fallen among his enemies, and must abide the issue of a terrible revenge.

By about the hour of half-past twelve they had reached a part of the road where, by the convenience of a slap, they could leave their equipage, with the donkey's neck fixed to a post, and his head within reach of some tempting provender. All this arranged to their satisfaction, they searched about for stray loungers, none of whom could be espied,—so straight they went to their destined work. As familiar with the burying-ground as they were with their own squalid dwellings, they were soon among the green hillocks, few of which, as they saw by the light of the moon, which came upon them in fitful gleams, making all these sombre things more like the productions of *feerie* than of honest nature, held out any temptations to these lovers of new sod. But at length the "Spune" stopped at an elevation more recent than any around it.

"This is the grave of Merrylees' father anyhow," said the superior.

"Then out with him," said the stolid Mowat.

"Still the idiot," said the other. "Did I not tell you last night he's gone into powder ten years ago, and that it's the sister we're after?"

"Then out wi' her," was the sulky reply.

Nor did the "Spune" need the stimulus of the stolid. He began straight the work,—difficult and arduous to all but such adepts,—puffing, and drawing wind to puff again.

"Hush!" said Mowat. "I heard a noise."

And the "Spune," who after all was a great coward, stood motionless to listen, but all was so still, even as the dead that lay around, that even the breathing of the men sounded like strong whispers. Then away wrought the reassured again, and anon the screwing, the jerking, the pulling, till at last came the final pull, shewing, in the passing beam, the long white shroud, with what it enveloped, extended on the green turf. At that moment the whole area rang with a shout, something between a roar and a yelp, and looking round they saw, behind a low head-stone, a tall figure in white (of course), with its long arms tossed up as with a sudden fling. The apparition was appalling even to men who had no more faith in ghosts than they had in souls; and just as another toss announced the coming shout, they took to flight, staggering as they flew over the numerous inequalities, but making more speed under the spur of terror than ever they had done under that of mammon. They were gone.

And now the apparition, after making some more strange movements, proceeded to take off a white sheet, which he deliberately stuck into the bottom of a coarse bag. Two or three giant steps brought him to the spoiled place of rest.

"And you're there, Sarah Merrylees?" he said, in a voice sufficiently hollow for the part he had so recently assumed. "The 'Spune' is without its porridge this time; and shall not man live on the fruit of the earth?"

And one might have fancied there was a chuckle, as if the creature had been satisfied with its own fun. But now came the part of this tragedy which will for certain be scouted as the work of fiction, but which as certainly made a part of the story. Merrylees,—for it was he, who, having met David Cameron of the West Port on the previous night, had learned the intention of his friends to visit Penicuik, and thereby came to the conclusion that his presence there would be useful,—then took out a rope, and, having gone through a process at which he was very expert, he was soon standing by the side of the wall under his burden of Sarah Merrylees. Nor was it long till he reached the high road, where, keeping by the dark side of the hedge, he intended to proceed to a convenient spot where he might leave his load till he could contrive to bring a conveyance. He had not proceeded far when he heard the roll of the cart, and saw his two friends alongside of it. There was no time to throw away over the head of such an opportunity. So, depositing his burden at the foot of the hedge, close by his side, he ran forward as far as was safe, crying out, "Stop the robbers!"—*Nestor Graecos objurgavit*; whereupon the terrified "Spune," with the white apparition still in his mind's eye, fled with renewed precipitation, closely followed by Mowat, and leaving David Cameron's cart with the donkey to whatever fate might overtake it. The coast being thus once more clear, and being well satisfied that his friends were too cowardly to return, he ran forward and stopped the donkey; then returning for his burden, he carried it to the cart, wherein he deposited it. A long sauntering journey brought him to town, where, after going through many manœuvres, he at last contrived to lodge his capture in the hall of the Square.

This terrible story—which, we may add, was a favourite among the students—was told by Merrylees, so far as pertained to him, as altogether applicable to another body, whereby he afforded proof that there is no hardness of heart to which man can attain that is utterly exclusive of a spot where some permeating feeling still supplies the issues of shame. About his part of it the "Spune" had small compunction; but, to confess the truth, it was not till we knew what occurred afterwards that we could bring ourselves to believe that it was possible for it to be true.

To those who know human nature, in the only proper way in which it can be known, it is scarcely necessary to say that we are always under the influence of that error which induces us to estimate the feelings of others by our own. But there is something about these judgments of others even more fallacious, in so far as it almost amounts to an impossibility that we can, through a feeling present, fancy the total absence of it in others. Unable to attain to a negative except in relation to the positive, through which it is thought to be seen, we must either project in some way the matter of our thoughts and feeling into the supposed non-existent, or not think at all. If we could suppose a total death of the affections in a brother as easily as the overwhelming domination of money, we would not deny credit to this most wonderful story; but there lies the difficulty, and you must get out of it the best way you can. Even if you don't succumb in despair, you are far still from the Court of Cacus, so soon to be opened to you by a pen, even as hell was opened to Virgil by the golden *ramus*.

RESUMPTION OF
THE GREAT DRAMA

The man whom, in our first chapter, we described as a neophyte, left the students with his bashfulness, if we can so call it, supplied by confidence. The power which we have already seen making such havoc among feelings and affections deemed all but ineradicable, had produced the first thrill in a heart long since dead to the pulses of pity. We may say so much, that his life, prior to this day—when there opened to him a vista through which he could see, amidst moving furies, the illuminated figure of mammon, with the means of getting money without hard labour—had been little else all through than a wrestle with poverty, often degenerating into squalid misery; and we may thus estimate the state of his mind, under the new-born hope of what, to such a man, might have the appearance of a small fortune.

But even with the view which the information given him by the students opened up of a new means of making money, we are not entitled to suppose that, as he that night directed his steps to the Cowgate with the intention of reaching the lodgings which he occupied in the West Port, he had any prevision of the extent to which this new pursuit would lead him. His expectations could only, as yet, be limited to the acquisition *in some way* of those objects required in the halls of the Square, and the value of which had previously come to his ears through the medium of that under-current of whispers to which the exploits of Merrylees, and the others then in the full progress of their career, had given impulse and meaning. Sure it was, at any rate, that he was utterly unconscious that he was permitted to be an agent, selected after due care by the devil, to push and force those passions by which a Christian country, with a name renowned throughout the world for virtue, had been scourged and scathed to a climax. Far less could he foresee the means—to our obscure vision of the ways of Providence—so out of proportion to the evils (already set forth by us) which they remedied, if not put an end to. So it has been said. But by what right do we make out that want of proportion? We know pretty nearly the amount of evil subsequently perpetrated by William Burke,—name of fear, and which even yet only passes in a whisper,—but we do not know (for all we have said is only an inkling,) and never will know, the amount of that other evil which his deeds were to be the means of bringing to an end. The cry had for years gone up to the great white throne of the outraged feelings of a Christian nation. There was only the exception of those who appealed to the pride of science, and man's natural love of life and a sound living body. Meanwhile, those in power, to whom Heaven had accorded the means of reconciliation, looked on with apathy, at least without interest,—an observation which may lead us to the thought that there was less of profanity than is generally supposed in the suggestion which some have ventured, and some have approved, that this man had a mission, yea, that the devil was permitted to tempt him to commit deeds which would rouse the country to seek a remedy sufficient to stop the violation of natural feelings, and at the same time provide for the claims of science.

So, with the sordid thoughts suited to his mission, he trudged along, looking about for some one he expected to see; and by and by there came from behind, and joined him, an individual, in the shape of a spare wretch, gruesome and goulish, of moderate height, with a cadaverous face, in which were set, in the most whimsical manner, two gray eyes, so far apart that it did not seem possible for him to look at you with both at the same time. There was in these oblique orbs, too, a leer which seemed to be the normal and unchangeable expression of a mind which not only disregarded the humanities and rights of his species, but mocked and laughed at them. Most creatures, even the wickedest, are at times surprised into moments of *bonhommie*. Nature seems to demand this as a kind of rest to the spirit, as if evil were a disturbance, which, to be sure, it generally is; but the malignity of this wonderful being was so thorough-going, smooth, and natural, that even what he might intend for a bastard kind of love or friendship was only a modification of his diabolism, so that his smile was merely a relaxation of his congenital enmity towards all that was good and beautiful in nature. This man was William Hare,—a name which, not less than that of William Burke, will ever be as an apparition to the retina of the ear of mankind.

The forgathering of these men was followed instantly, but secretly, as if they feared the chances of a whisper having a collateral fall, by the reciprocation of confidences, in which, as a matter of course, was included the success of the visitor to the Square, and over the face of the listener there came merely a stronger phase of the ordinary expression of the malign pleasure which less or more always played in those divergent eyes. But these conferences cannot be understood without a knowledge of what had taken place in the latter's house in Tanners' Close, to which they were loungingly directing their steps, and where the former lodged. And many others lodged there too, for it was one of those low caravanseries or lodging-houses which are as well the refuge of trampers, who would pass there a night, as of more permanent residenters, who, deprived of a home by vagabondism, earned a desultory livelihood as chance carriers or troggan-mongers, fish-hawkers, or peripatetic dealers in small wares. Sometimes a lodger a little above these classes would find his account in the cheap refuge, and three days before that night a tall man, a pensioner, who ordinarily went by the name of Donald, had died, a short time only before his pension became due. To that pension the master of the establishment had looked forward as the means of being reimbursed for several months' rent and advances, amounting to somewhere about £4. This loss rankled in the mind of Hare, for though Donald was not without some poor friends who would see him decently buried, they were without the means, as well perhaps the will, to pay a debt for the justice of which the bad character of the creditor could be no guarantee.

And here we have the best evidence, that even on that day when Donald died, and up to the morning of the funeral, and eight or ten hours previous to this forgathering in the Cowgate, no thought had crossed the mind of either of these men of taking the debt out of the body of the pensioner. Allowing for all discrepancies as to the time when the tongue of one of them gave expression to the dark purpose, it is clear that the communication would not, on the supposition of the thought having been slumbering in the mind, have been delayed till the morning of the funeral, nor even to the hour of bringing in the coffin. No doubt they had been both aware that such things had been done, and were being done, in Edinburgh at that time, and the temptation had crossed them, not without being accepted by their sordidness. The intention and the thought sprang up together, and, by all accounts, it was the mind of Hare that produced the birth; but the exclusiveness of the *credit* was just so much the less in proportion to the readiness by which it was on the instant adopted and cherished by his friend. You may here mark an analogy, which it might be of pregnant interest for all men, and women too, to ponder, as a *little* sermon, and not the less that this entire history is a *big* one:—The tiny seed will lie in the ground for years, and though the soil may be known to be congenial in the wealth of rottenness, it will not spring to the expectation of the gardener. It may be tossed over and over, and hither and thither for years, and appear above ground, shooting resolutely its stem, when not only not looked for, but against all expectation. So it is with the mind and its germs. The small shoot of an invention takes its start from an agreement of circumstances unknown to us, and grows and grows into branching horrors; nay, every branch, and leaflet, and poisonous calyx has its secondary origin in a germ as mysteriously stimulated as the one that lay so long perhaps in the earth. And what then? Why, just this—that our practical philosophy is ever vexing itself by tugging at the cords of Calvinism. Why and how did this thought arise in the mind of Hare? Because he was a wicked man. And why was he a wicked man? The old story of the scroll, whereon were marked in fire the names of the reprobates. But reject it, and say that he made himself a wicked man. Try that process upon yourself, if you happen to be a good one, or the opposite, if you happen to be bad, and see how you will succeed by such decree of your own.

The proposition was thus made that the body of the stalwart Donald should be sold to the doctors, and at once agreed to by the listener, only with the scruple that there was no time between the period of their conversation and the funeral to get all matters arranged—a sorry objection from such a man, and so accordingly made small account of by either. And so they straightway set about getting the bag of tanner's bark—a circumstance which shews us that the practices of Merry-Andrew and his brethren had reached their ears. Nor are we to have the smallest hesitation in assuming that Helen M'Dougal, with whom Burke lived in concubinage, and Hare's wife—the two females in the house—joined to form that quatern destined to the orgies of the Court of Cacus. The bag of bark was speedily procured, the body of Donald hauled out of the coffin and deposited on a bed, the bark was put in, the lid screwed down, and all made decent and fair for the bearers. When the vice has fructified into an act, how easy is the tribute paid to virtue! And so these men, according to the normal course, joined with long faces the train of the mourners, among whom—though some of them who loved the jolly old pensioner had tears in their eyes—they could hold up, or rather down, their faces as mournfully as the best.

The interlude of this play of the forenoon, and the melodrama of the night, consisted in the appearance of Burke in the hall in Surgeons' Square, and having forgathered in the Cowgate in the manner we have set forth, the two friends, bound together by prior confidences, of which no man ever knew the extent or nature, pursued their way to Tanners' Close, where they were welcomed by the women with the remainder of the whisky got for the funeral. The offering was to nerve them for the work in which they were merely apprentices; nor was the offering given and participated in less cheerfully by the women themselves, that they had both applied the soft hand of feminine attentions to the gallant pensioner,—even hung over his squalid couch tenderly, and wet his dry lips, and all the more, surely, that he had been a soldier, had seen and mixed in battles in his day, and therefore deserved something better than a bag for a winding sheet, and the knife of the anatomist coming after, at so long a distance, the bayonet of the enemy. Such gilt, which shews itself everywhere as society gets more civilised, is easily rubbed off; and with the knowledge of these tender nurses, the two men proceeded to their work, which, coarse as it was, was easily executed. The bag was filled and hoisted on the shoulders of Burke, who carried it in the dark as far as Bristo Port, where Hare, as a relay, took up the burden. So well known along the Grassmarket and Cowgate, where their figures might have excited attention, they took then the round-about way of College Street, and, getting to the Square, they felt some of that hesitation—shall we call it bashfulness?—which Burke had betrayed at his prior visit. They accordingly placed their load at the door of a cellar in the lower part of the buildings, and mounting to the room where one of them had been before, encountered the same three young assistants still engaged in their ardent work.

"Bring it up," was the reply of more than one, when they had heard the words of the merchants, as they hung fire in their mouths and tongues. Up soon *it* was, and drawn out and laid upon the table in the winding-sheet. Yes, a piece of delicacy that which was soon to be dispensed with as extravagant and unnecessary. And the covering partially drawn off, there is that rapid and curious, yet never perfectly composed, scanning of the eyes of even old students, but with no recoil on the part of the sellers, who had sat and drank with the old soldier, and heard his stories of Peninsular battles, and laughed at his jokes. Not the less racy these, that he thought his companions kind and jolly souls—how far away from the intention of selling his body for gold he never imagined, for the idea could not have entered the mind of Suspicion herself, if there be any such goddess in the mythology of poets. But all such reminiscences, if they threatened to force an entry into the minds of these men, were quickly sent back to the limbo of obliviousness by the obdurate mammon.

By and by, and after the exit of one of the students, there came in the monoculus himself, Knox, and the covering was altogether withdrawn. It seemed to him a fair mercantable commodity. That is, it was not too old for any of the valuable tissues,—in the midst of which lay the secrets these students were so anxious to reveal, not for the purpose of filling their pockets in after-times, but for the benefit of mankind,—to have been dissolved or injured. Seven pounds ten shillings is pronounced as the price of the body of the veteran. A shadow passed over the faces of the sellers; the sum did not come up to the hopes inspired by the reports which had oozed out of the earnings of the Merry-Andrews and the "Spunes." Yet the sum, to these wretched earners of pennies for vagrants' beds and cobbled shoes, was a *coup* of mammon sufficient to have made their hardened hearts clatter upon their ribs, and scare away the last trace of humanity inspired by the lips of a mother, kept otherwise, and up to this time, unscathed by the temptations of the devil. But they could not refuse the sum,—that is, they had not yet hardihood to chaffer; and, the money being paid, they were on the eve of departing, when they were told that they would be made welcome again, if they came with an equally good recommendation. And as they went, they did not forget the shirt.

So, with the first spoil in his pocket—for Burke was the foremost man, and got the money—he and his friend betook themselves to Tanners' Close, keeping, no doubt, in remembrance, the words of the students, that they would be welcome again. Nor can we have any doubt that when they arrived at home, after a day of such novel and ingenious, and, we may surely add, triumphant performance, they would celebrate, with the women, in an orgie debauch of hours, this great event of a new birth of hope, the realisation of which would elevate them even to an upper caste among the humble inhabitants of Portsburgh. But even they themselves did not know what progeny would come of this cockatrice's egg, laid in the dark corner of the habitation of sin. Our story would not have carried that moral, which is the eternal burden of all histories of crime, if the thought of murder had come to them without that prelusive conciliation, under the condition of which the devil is permitted to arrive at his greatest achievements.

Much, even at this early stage, was made of the conduct of Knox and his assistants, but, we think, with little justice to these men. Why did they not ask those dark and suspicious-looking ruffians, who did not belong to their regular staff, where they got the object thus brought to them? The answer appears to be satisfactory, whatever might be thought of their subsequent defence and explanations. There was nothing here to excite suspicion, except, as it was said, the absence of certain marks often made by resurrectionists in their process of working, but the exception went for nothing in the face of an assertion that such marks are seldom to be seen; and then, as for the asserted naturalness—if we may use the expression of an inquiry of such a kind—it was said, and may be repeated, that that which appears to be natural is not always expedient. We are here to keep in view that the medical men were aware that they were dealing in smuggled goods, the participation on their part being, as they conceived, justified by the necessities of their profession; and when was it ever known that the dealer with a smuggler questioned him as to the whereabouts and the manner of his contravention of the laws? It does not need even to be remarked, that to discourage is not the best way to lay the foundation of a new bargain; nay, there was weight in the observation, that the prudent avoidance of such interrogation had become a habit, and though they were perfectly aware that bodies had been brought to them which had never been in graves, and, consequently, that there existed a practice of sale and purchase between the men devoted to this profession, and the friends or distant relatives of the dead, they still considered that all such cases were covered by the claims of science, whereby society got returned to it, in the shape of an increased knowledge and skill of cure, that which had been taken from it against the sanction of human affections. Then it was admitted, even by the "howlers," that never, up to this time, had there been offered a body which could be said to have borne marks of violence; and if the minds of at least these generous and well-bred youths never entertained a suspicion of murder, the fact might more properly have been adduced as honourable to their estimate of mankind, than as an objection to their want of guard against an evil which had not yet appeared in the world, and which was to become, unhappily, in good old Scotland, a new species of crime.

THE QUATERNION

We suspect there is scarcely a life of a great man, whether he has been great for good or for evil, in which you will not find passages that are analogous to some things in your own. As with the physical monsters, described by such men as Dr Denham, in which there is always a natural foundation out of which grow the amorphous excrescences which we call monstrosities, so in the moral there is always something that pertains to the natural, insomuch that we may say, that the abnormal beings who go by the name of monsters are, as respects their unenvied peculiarity, the result of a twist in the development of what was intended to be according to the ordinary rule. The observation may serve as a *cave diabolum* even to those who think they are for certain out of the reprobatory decrees.

William Burke was born in the parish of Orrey, county of Tyrone, Ireland, in the spring of 1792. When at school, he was distinguished as an apt scholar, and was, besides, cleanly and active in his habits. Though bred a Catholic, he was taken when very young into the service of a Presbyterian minister, a circumstance which may explain the religious tendencies he subsequently exhibited; but even at this early period, he began to shew signs of that versatility of purpose which, leading sometimes to success, more often ends in vagabondism. Having left the minister to try the trade of a baker, he renounced that for the occupation of a weaver; and from that he enlisted in the Donegal militia. Yet in the midst of these changes he observed so much moral regularity that he was selected by one of the officers as his servant. While thus employed he married a young woman in Ballinha; and after seven years he returned to live with her, on the disbanding of the regiment. Still with a fair character, he then became the servant to a neighbouring gentleman, with whom he lived three years. Meanwhile he had a family by his wife; and having taken it into his head that he would be able to maintain them by getting a sub-lease of a piece of ground from his father-in-law, who was himself a tenant, he insisted for this right, which was refused, and the quarrel which ensued sent him to Scotland. Still, however, even in his advanced manhood, without any other stain than an imputed infidelity to his wife, we are assured, at least, that as yet he had shewn no indications of what may be termed cruelty even by the fastidious, if it was not that he bore the reputation of mildness approaching to softness.

Yet he came to Scotland with this blot on his soul, and it was soon deepened, when, having gone to work as a labourer on the Union Canal, he fell in, at Meddiston, with Helen M'Dougal, a comely, if not good-looking, young widow, then residing there after the death of her husband. It has been always said that this was an affair of love, at least it ended in a connexion so close that they resolved to live together.

It would appear that the connexion thus formed having been communicated to his priest, he was admonished, and recommended to return to his wife; and a consequence of his refusal was the ordinary excommunication. Yet he continued to have religious fits, during the continuance of which he avoided the chapel, from the terrors of the anathema. We trace him afterwards, as he returned with his paramour to Edinburgh, where he fell, as the consequence of his continued versatility, into peripatetic pedlery, buying and vending old clothes, skins of animals, human hair, and other small articles and wares. Nor did he stick by this, soon betaking himself to cobbling, for which, in a rude way, he discovered that he had a turn, though he had never been taught the craft; and by purchasing old shoes and boots, to which he applied his art, and getting M'Dougal to hawk them, he contrived to realise fifteen or twenty shillings a-week. At this time he was a lodger in "*The Beggars' Hotel,*" kept by the well-known Mikey Culzean,—an establishment which had a famous termination, when, being one day burned to the ground, there came forth, driven by the flames, such a swarm of beggars, halt and blind, that their congregation seemed as difficult to account for as the assemblage of a colony of rats. Among them appeared Burke and M'Dougal; but there were left behind in the fire the library of the cobbler, consisting of Ambrose's "Looking unto Jesus," Boston's "Fourfold State," "The Pilgrim's Progress," and Booth's "Reign of Grace." Once more he became a lodger with Mikey, who took up a new hotel in Brown's Close, Grassmarket.

That the man, originally neither cruel nor profane, was not yet, like Balaam, left to his idol, would appear from his continued religious exercises. The grace of the Lord tracks the devil in his darkest caves. In the next house the candle of salvation burned, and even cast its light into the thick atmosphere of the surrounding dens. Thither Burke repaired, and joined, with apparent seriousness, in the exercise of devotion; nor did he fail to tax the incurable Mikey with profanity, when that notorious lover of a joke, even at the expense of divine things, thrust his head through the papered partition, and cried out, to the dismay of the devotees, "The performance is just going to begin." In all this there seemed to be no hypocrisy, because there was no use to which he tried to turn it; and then his conversations on the subject of the service, which, after the company dispersed, he had with the man in whose house the meetings were held, seemed to be too secret for the displays of the mere dissembler.

Other traits conspired to shew the nature of the man, before the temptations of the idol changed it. Kind and serviceable, inoffensive and playful, he was industrious as well, and seldom inclined for drink. Fond of singing and playing on the flute, he sought, in his melancholy moods, the solace of plaintive airs. All which qualities were combined with a jocular and quizzical turn, which, displaying a fund of low humour, made him a favourite. Some anecdotes are given in illustration,—as where, one day, when he heard a salt-wife bawling out, "Wha'll buy salt?" he replied, "Upon my word, I doun't know; but if you ask that woman gaping at the door opposite, perhaps she may inform you;" or where, on another, when, having been abused by a painted Jezebel on the High Street, he tried to shame her by an accusation: "I might have passed over the painting," said he, "if it had been properly done, but it's shameful to come to the street bedaubed in that unskilful way,"—an objurgation which was applauded by the bystanders.

Yet, withal, there were deductions to be made from such favourable accounts, inducing the conviction that there is small faith due to drawn characters, where, perhaps, the potentialities may have been asleep, only awaiting the touch of the demon. But is not this less or more the case with all of us? if it be not metaphysically true that every unregenerated man has his price,—that is, every such man has a sacrifice of moral principle to sell, if a price and a purchaser can be found to his liking. What a million of money will not purchase, may be bought by the smile or tear of a woman. The paradox cannot be disproved, because the eventualities of temptation cannot be exhausted in any one man's life. This man, though appearing to have kindly feelings, could be cruel to the woman who, whatever her faults, had followed him in all his wanderings and misery; but then, of course, there was *the occasion*, as where, having roused her jealousy by attentions to a young woman who was related to her, he, in return for her complaints, almost murdered her. The story current at the time was, that the three having slept in the same bed, the quarrel began between the two women, who, betaking themselves to the floor, entered into a battle. So long as the conflict was maintained on nearly equal terms, the man contented himself with witnessing it; but when the elder virago was likely to master the young one, he rose out of bed, and interfered in behalf of the latter. His interference soon turned the scale; and he inflicted an unmerciful punishment upon his partner. Then came the neighbours, who found M'Dougal extended upon the floor apparently lifeless, with the man standing by, and contemplating. After some time she exhibited signs of life, when again seizing her by the hair, he cried, "There is life in her yet!" and dashed her head violently on the floor. By this time the police were attracted by the noise, who, upon asking Burke whether the woman was his wife, got the reply in a mild, if not insinuating tone, "Yes, gentlemen, she is my wife."

We thus get to one of the secrets of this man's character. The passions are said to occur in opposite phases—strong loves, and strong hatreds, and so forth; but there is one which nature, in love, has reserved, pure, solitary, and unchangeable, without counterpart to dim its lustre, or antagonist to neutralise its effect, and that is *pity*. This man wanted pity. If we were fanciful, we might here go with the gentle poets, who tell us, in their way, that, like the dew-drop which falls in the evening, and shines equally clear on the deadly nightshade and the rose, it solaces virtue in adversity, without scorning sin in the pains of retribution. If, in our analysis of man's character, we find not his heart, as the fire-opal, enclosing one of nature's tears, we may throw the crucible aside, extinguish the fire, and cast the *caput mortuum* to the dogs; and yet dogs have pity. We have found, even already, enough to lead us to another clue. He possessed radical cunning, the greatest and most insuperable of all the obstacles to moral and religious emendation. Other evils only hang about the heart, but this, the true gift of the devil, is the very blood of the organ. We are, then, led to suspect him of religious hypocrisy. If we were not told there is hope for all, we might surely say that the advent of the Spirit of grace is possible in every case but that of hypocrisy veiled by religion; yea, the creature cursed with this vice, Faith views in the distance as an impossibility, and flies past in despair, to try her persuasions on the *honest* sinner.

The subsequent notices of this man's life, up to the commencement of the deeds which have rendered him famous, only tend to confirm these observations. Renouncing once more his cobbling, he went, still followed by his partner, to

Peebles, where he was employed in road-making. Though still maintaining some pretensions to religion, he now began to shew a gradual deterioration of character, keeping suspicious hours, and making his house the resort of profligate characters, where scenes of drunkenness and riot were of common occurrence, especially on Saturday nights and Sundays. Retaining the same vagrant habits, he next betook himself to Penicuik, and after the harvest of 1827, still accompanied by M'Dougal, he came once more to reside in Edinburgh, where the occasion offered of getting acquainted with Hare, and becoming a lodger with him in his house in Tanner's Close, called Log's lodgings. This house, which afforded room for seven beds, was kept under the name of Mrs Hare's first husband, Log, and being the resort of all kinds of loose wanderers, washed off from the lowest bed of the conglomerates, was the scene of still greater riots than the lodger had ever patronized in his own. That the intimacy between him and his landlord had soon ripened into such friendship as these people are capable of, was proved by an occurrence mentioned by a person who called on Burke with the intention of giving him a job. He found Hare beating without mercy his friend's paramour, who was extended on the floor, while Burke was sitting unconcernedly at the window. When asked why he allowed another man to beat his wife, "Oh, she deserves all she is getting," was the reply. Yet the man still preserved more of a respectable character than those with whom he here associated—retaining even yet much of his disposition to serve, his quiet humour, if not a species of politeness, all of which was perfectly reconcilable with the presence of that potentiality of crime which lay slumbering in the heart, under the thin veil of religion, and not to be crossed or checked, when roused to action, by pity, no trace of which appeared to be in him. He was set aside for his idol, and only waited the temptation to become what he became.

William Hare, the second of our quaternion, was also a native of Ireland, having been born in the neighbourhood of

Londonderry. Like so many of the poor children of that country, he was never trained to any trade whereby he might have been saved from that gradual descent into desultory modes of earning a livelihood, which leading, as we have already said, to vagabondism, is the introduction to so many temptations. After working at country work for some time near his native place, he came over to Scotland, where he engaged as a common labourer upon the Union Canal, and assisted for some time in the work of unloading Mr Dawson's boats at Port-Hopetoun. It was here that he became acquainted with Log or Logue, to whose widow he was subsequently married, and with whom he came to lodge. After the canal was finished, he betook himself to the occupation of a travelling huckster, going about the country with an old horse and cart, selling at one time fish, at another crockery, or exchanging the latter for old iron, which he disposed of to the dealers. From the cart and the horse he went down to the hurley, using that vehicle for much the same purposes. Some quarrel with Log, before the latter's death, drove him to new quarters; but not long after, and when Log had been dead and buried, he returned to Tanner's Close, where he assumed all the rights of the landlord of seven beds, as well as the privileges of the husband, though Mrs Log was never called by his name.

It was now that, having tasted power in becoming a landlord with such drawings as twopence or threepence a night, he shewed more of his character than had previously been known. Always inclined to take drink, wherever and whenever he could get it, he now, as a consequence of idleness and opportunity, became drunken and dissolute—the effect of liquor being to render him quarrelsome and always ready to fight. Nay, so strong was this propensity in him, that he appeared always to be on the outlook for a contest, picking a quarrel upon any opportunity, and even trying to make one out of the simple act of looking at him. Though a sorry pugilist, he had no fear of an opponent twice his size, and never gave in until fairly disabled—even then endeavouring to wreak, in so far as oaths could, a vengeance on the head of his enemy. On the failure of an opponent without, he had no difficulty, so long as Mrs Log was there, of finding one within; nor was she, also a drunkard, loath to encounter him upon equal terms, so that the house was seldom free from brawls, if it did not often exhibit a regularly-contested battle between the master and mistress. Even vice has its traits of ludicrousness. Those of the neighbours who were fond of sights were often enough gratified by some wag going and reporting to the landlady that Willie Hare, as he was usually called, was upon the street drunk, whereupon the wife, herself probably in the same state, would issue forth in search of him, when a battle was the issue of the rencontre. Such was the kind of life led by this couple up to the time of Burke's entry.

The passion of violence produced by inebriation will not always, or indeed often, afford any clue to character. It may be hardly necessary to say that Hare was naturally cruel, yet we have seen that Burke could scarcely be said to present that feature unless when roused by some strong motive, so that we have no difficulty in finding at the first glance an essential difference in the two men;—the one being, in his very nature and constitution, vindictive and malign—the other ready to suffocate the humanity that was in him at the beck of an impulse strong enough to move him. Only one of them could probably have been guilty of such an action as this: On one occasion, when a person of the name of M'Lean (the narrator) was returning from shearing at Carnwath, he got into company with Hare, Burke, and his wife, and the party went into a public-house at Balerno, near Currie, to get some refreshment. When the reckoning was, as they call it, clubbed, Hare snatched up the money from the table and pocketed it, whereupon Burke, in the fear of a disturbance, advanced the sum. On leaving the inn, M'Lean taxed the offender with his trick, who, in place of being ashamed or even pocketing the affront, knocked the feet from his companion, laid him on the ground, and kicked him with his shoe pointed with iron plates. If we add to this inborn malignity which, in feeling, whether expressed by words or acts, arrayed him against mankind, and scarcely ever alleviated by those emotions of friendship which are to be found in the most hardened breasts, that scorn of human nature, not unaccompanied with satirical laughter, to which we have alluded, we have that foundation of character in the man upon which was so easily reared the towering edifice of his crimes.

Yet after all this information, which was so industriously gleaned, the psychologist was not satisfied. He wanted to vindicate human nature from even a possible diverging incidence of a law which could account for such crimes, by tracing them to malignity and mammon. We would fain look with favour on such scepticism; and it is to be admitted that all who had the curiosity to see and converse with this man discovered a want. With a low animal brow, he justified the phrenologist by discovering no power of ratiocination, if, indeed, what is termed reasoning was not an impossibility to him. His mind was entirely under the government of external objects, among which selfishness made its selection, irrespective of the humanities, of which he had none. We might thus term him, as he has been called, a fool or semi-idiot, only within the limits of that responsibility which the law is bound, for the preservation of mankind, to push far beyond the verge where nature draws her distinctions between the morally sane and the insane. We thus get quit of the heavy imputation which the doings of such a man cast upon our kind; and if we are met by the reflection, that Burke had both thought and sense to an extent which was rather a surprise to those who conversed with him with a view to ascertain the structure of his mind, we have the advantage of the reply, that, naturally indolent, if not soft, he allowed himself to be ruled by another, who, with all his defects, possessed resolution and a dominating will. The history of mankind is full of the phenomena of "imposed will"—the source of more divergence from the normal line than we ever dream of.

We come now to the third of our quaternion, Helen M'Dougal,

a native, as we have said, of the small village of Meddiston, in the parish of Muiravonside, and county of Stirling, where her early years were spent. Her maiden name was Dougal. At no time, however early, did her character exhibit any such diversity of oscillation between the good and the evil, as, giving play to contending passions, creates an interest in the inquirer into human nature. All seemed to be straight, on and down from the beginning. At an early period she formed a connexion with a man, M'Dougal, who resided in the same village, to whom she bore a child during the lifetime of his wife. After the latter's death, the intercourse which continued led to cohabitation, passing for marriage, and she bearing his name. Afterwards coming together to Leith, where he followed his occupation of a sawyer, she was left alone, poor and friendless, by his death, which took place from typhus while he was confined in Queensberry House. She now returned to her native village, where she met with Burke, then, as we have seen, a labourer on the canal, when that intercourse commenced, the evil auspices of which were to be so terribly verified. Thereafter, wherever they resided, there seems never to have been much change in the character of this woman. In Edinburgh, Leith, Peebles, or Penicuik, she was always distinguished for loose and drunken habits; nor were these ever relieved by any geniality of nature, the uniform expression of her mind and countenance being a stern moroseness which concentrated upon her universal dislike, so that it was often said that she was unworthy even of Burke. From all this it may easily be induced that she was not, in the crimes of which she was cognisant, or in which she took a part, under any influence of an imposed will on the part of Burke; the contrary being rather to be presumed, that she ruled him, and that it was only when he was roused by her fierceness of temper or jealousy that he repaid her domination by a cruel punishment.

The last of the four, Margaret Laird or Hare, was, like her husband, a native of Ireland, and accompanied her first husband, Log, to Scotland. The latter bore the character of a decent, hard-working man, who had not only the world out of doors to contend with, but within, the temper of a masculine wife. Some success enabled him to become a small contractor on the Union Canal, and for some time he worked his contract, with a detachment of his countrymen, in the neighbourhood of Winchburgh; but we may estimate the extent of his contract, and not less the Irish peculiarity of both the man and his wife, when we know that the contractor's lady worked along with the men in the character of a labourer, with a man's coat on her back, wheeling a barrowful of rubbish as stoutly as any of her men. At that time, they inhabited a temporary hut on the banks of the canal, and, whatever her faults may have been, she exhibited here nothing but economy and industry. The work being finished, Log settled in Edinburgh, where, though honest enough, the contractor became sunk in the huckster, and the keeper of a beggars' hotel, which was soon to rival even Mickey Culzean's. Upon his death, the lodging and furniture, such as it was, with any small earnings he had saved, devolved upon the widow, and thereafter she conducted the establishment; but she soon shewed the smallness of her gratitude and the strength of her passion by cohabiting with one of her lodgers, described as young and good-looking, and, thereafter, the depravity of her taste in accepting Hare after the young lover forsook her. Yet her choice was only that which is made by those who seek their kind. The drunkard and semi idiot had charms for one who was herself destitute not less of virtue than of prudence, and we are soon to see her descending into unparalleled crime, not by the imposed will of Hare, but the ready suggestion of her own heart.

Such are the characters of our wonderful story; and we make no apology to sensible men for disentombing such specimens of our kind from the dust-covered chronicles of their deeds. A salutary horror, not only of their great crimes, but also of those lesser ones which led to these, pervaded the people of Scotland long after the tragedy of so many acts and scenes was performed; and thus it is, in the providence of God, that virtue becomes brighter by the contrast with vice. It is only, as some one has observed, when the tempest tosses the waves of the ocean into mountains that we see into its depths. It was by the light of burning Troy that Æneas saw the faces of the gods; and so it is through the light of human passions that we discover the nature of the heart of man.

THE OPENING
OF THE COURT

THE OLD WOMAN OF GILMERTON [5]

The house which went by the name of Log's lodging-house, and which was occupied by William Hare, as raised by the favour of the widow to the elevation of landlord, was, as already said, situated in Tanner's Close,—one of those narrow passages that wind from the north side of the West Port. The entry from the street begins with a descent of a few steps, and is dark from the superincumbent land. On proceeding downwards, you came—for the house, which was rased for shame, is no longer to be seen—to a smallish self-contained dwelling of one flat, and consisting of three apartments. One passing down the close might, with an observant eye, have seen into the front room; but this disadvantage was compensated by the house being disjoined from other dwellings, and a ticket, "Beds to let," as an invitation to vagrants, so many of whom were destined never to come out alive, distinguished it still more. The outer apartment was large, occupied all round by these structures called beds, composed of knocked-up fir stumps, and covered with a few gray sheets and brown blankets, among which the squalid wanderer sought rest, and the profligate snored out his debauch under the weight of nightmare. Another room opening from this was also comparatively large, and furnished much in the same manner. In place of any concealment being practised, so far impossible, indeed, in the case of a public lodging-house, the door stood generally open, and, as we have said, the windows were overlooked by the passengers up and down; but as the spider's net is spread open while his small keep is a secret hole, so here there was a small apartment, or rather closet, the window of which looked upon a pig-sty and a dead wall, and into which, as we know, were introduced those unhappy beings destined to death. The very character of the house, the continued scene of roused passions, saved it from that observation which is directed towards temporary tumults, so that no surprise could have been excited by cries of suffering issuing from such a place, even if they could have been heard from the interior den; and that was still more impossible, from the extraordinary mode of extinguishing life adopted by the wary and yet unwary colleagues. In this inner apartment Burke used to work when he did work, which, always seldom, soon came to be rare, and eventually relinquished for other wages.

It will thus be seen that this small dark room was the appropriate place where the words of secrecy would pass to the ear, or be blurted forth, coarse and broken, under the fevered brain of drunkenness. Since ever that night when the £7, 10s. flared its magnetic influence over their eyes, and was communicated, by confidence and sympathy, to the two females, the little world of this quaternity was changed. The women saw that other lodgers would die, and the inspiring hope, not so demoniac as to curdle the remaining drops of human kindness that refused to leave the female breast, pointed in the inevitable direction of gaudy finery, which they might flaunt in the wondering eyes of the poor people of Portsburgh; but so slow a process did not suit the inflamed passions of the men. Hare had been revolving in his mind a scheme to set up his own will as the arbiter of the occasion, which would secure more money, even as he wished it; and the secret of this talisman behoved to be communicated to his friend, now poor and miserable, and dissolved in habits of sloth and inebriety. It was in that small room, and while the two women were engaged in the front apartments, that this mystic rite was performed between the solitary inmates, over, as might be expected, the caldron fires of drink. Yes, the mouth found power to utter the words which came as the dictates of a mere desire for money, that they should seize the opportunity so often presented to them of people lying drunk and senseless, and deprive them, by suffocation, of life. The proposition was accepted under the same approving auspices of mammon, who had already made both his own; and under the force of that temptation involved in the words which had been uttered in Surgeon's Square, offering a welcome to a return with a similar burden to that of the pensioner. You may cease to indulge here in those visions of the fancy which would represent human nature in convulsions, panting under the impression of a thought which, at first, produced a revolt, and then became conciliated. The "make" of each of these men was perfect under its own conditions, and if there was any seriousness, it was only a passing fear that they might bring their necks into jeopardy. Pity, which never lived in them, could not be said to be dead; the impress of the first money had burned into their souls; the welcome of the doctors rung in their ears; and Grace, studying them in the distance, had flown past them as an impossibility.

There is reason to believe that this resolution come to by these men, sitting together in this dark room, passed as an element into an orgy, different from all those in which they had so often indulged, if not from any that the world ever witnessed; nor was it modified, if it was not inflamed, by those visions of struggling nature expiring among their hands, which, rising as mere spectral forms, disappeared as soon before the images they pictured of a life of sensual indulgence and enervating sloth. If the project had sprung out of the ebullitions of intoxicated passions, it might have died away on the morrow, but, the result of calculation, it only received strength from the hopes which it roused, and which again were inflamed by the celebration. Nay, time, as day by day passed without a likely lodger coming in, increased the desire to begin, and chafed them into impatience. Hare accordingly resolved to commence prowling about the streets for some promising individual whom he might seduce into the house, and for some days he followed this occupation, but his efforts failed, and the report at night only again inflamed the desire of the morning. One afternoon, it was in December 1827, he again betook himself to the street, and for hours dodged about searching among the poor and miserable for some one who, already intoxicated, might offer those facilities to a beginner which were afterwards held of small account when practice gave proficiency and success confidence. At last he observed in the Grassmarket a decent-looking elderly woman (Abigail Simpson, as afterwards ascertained) whose wandering eye and irregular step shewed that she had got more of the publican's drug than her perhaps weak head could carry. His eye was immediately fixed upon her, and the old smile, which always obeyed the bidding of an evil thought, played over his face, nor did he let her out of his sight as he dogged her irregular movements from place to place. He could see that she was poor, that she was probably friendless, and, above all, that she was tipsy, and he knew enough of degraded nature to tell him what the proverb has settled, *Qui a bu boira*,—he who has drunk will drink more. Making up to her, he introduced himself as one who had met her before, and to his delight, discovered that she was inclined to be communicative, if not garrulous. It was not a difficult matter to advise her to accompany him to his house, where he would treat her with the old bribe of "a dram." So away they trudged together, the dissembler taking special care as he went to keep her on her course, from which she was every moment inclined to stray, by professions of interest and friendship.

Arrived at the lodging-house, the woman was introduced to Burke, with what looks between the two may easily be imagined, as an old friend, and drink was immediately procured. There was now a party which was joined by the two women, who, when they saw the men plying the stranger with whisky—the full value of which their difficulty in getting it to the extent they desired was sufficiently known to them—must have been aware that there was at the bottom of this generosity more than the friendship professed by men dead to the feeling, even as regards those who might have had a claim to it. The time passed, and the party became merry, nor was the stranger the least joyous of them, for had she not fallen among friends by sheer accident? and should she not prove her gratitude by being happy, ay, and communicating to them all her secrets? Was she not fortunate in being able to tell them that she was a pensioner of a gentleman in the New Town, who paid her regularly one shilling and sixpence a-week, besides little gratuities, such as the can of kitchen-fee she carried with her, and put aside till she should depart? Yes, and more, that she was blessed with a fine young daughter she had left at home, and who would be anxiously waiting her return. And then that daughter was not only good, she was *beautiful*, and the very pride of her soul. All this Hare heard; and he could carry out the play she had begun, even amidst the intentions he entertained, by expressing an interest in the mother's paragon, so deeply felt, that, being unmarried, he would put in for her hand, provided the mother would consent. And consent she did, so far as her condition would allow, and here, newly forged, was another bond of friendship. Nay, when he and the daughter should have become man and wife, it behoved that they could not live without the good old mother—who, accordingly, would take up her residence with them, with no more cares of poverty, and no dependence upon the pensioning gentleman of the New Town.

Could any human creature be more happy? Nor were the actors less so, though for a reason so very different. But the drink went done, even with the forbearance of the men, that she who would pay so dearly for it should have enough for their purpose. Mrs Hare had money, and there was the can of kitchen-fee, which the stranger could sell, and take home with her—*when the time came*—the price, one and sixpence, to help her little pension, and get a dram at another time, when they would not be there to give it to her. Then, to make the play even more merry and ingenious, this small sum was, very soon after, again, taken from the now almost unconscious woman's pocket, and laid out on more spirits, that the expected opportunity might be made more propitious. The scene progressed with even increased symptoms of noisy merriment. The old woman revived, and, under so many influences bearing on a kindly heart, did her best to sing some of her old songs—household words to her, no doubt, and feelings as well, with which she often at home wiled back the days of her youth, and charmed the ear of that daughter of whom she was so proud and so fond. Nay, we have the hearsay of the day for saying, that Burke contributed his part, singing, as he was so much in the habit of doing, some of those airs, generally, according to the account of those who knew him, sentimental, if not melancholy.

And here we are obliged absolutely to stop for a moment, not that we wish to intrude upon the reader a moralising spirit, where every word suggests a sermon out of more hardened things than stones, but that we are mystified, and are inclined to ask counsel. Could that man have had any sense of the beautiful in the sentiments of these lyrics which, it was said, he sang with feeling, if not pathos? Can it be possible that such a sense can be consistent with a demoralisation such as his? We suspect that it is. We are led to expect its impossibility by a reference to opposite, if not antagonistic, feelings: we cannot love and hate the same object. This is true, and would seem to disprove our proposition *à priori*. We can reconcile the contradiction only by having recourse to the different faculties of the imagination and the sense. The poet who has ravished his readers by a description of the beauty of female virtue and innocence has been found in a brothel. One of the most touching religious poems in the world has been sung by one who, among brawling revellers, maligned religion and its votaries. The praises of temperance have been enchantingly poured forth by a bacchanal. The oppressor of the poor has wept at a representation of affecting generosity. Any one may fill up the list without perhaps including a hypocrite. The imagination has its emotions, and the sense its feelings, or, perhaps, no feelings. The why and the wherefore touch the ultimate, and we are lost; but the fact remains, as proved by evidence, that William Burke could, in song, be pathetic.

Recurring to our real tragedy, the effect of the drink soon again sent the creature from her lyrics into a condition which might have suited the purpose of the men; but whether it was that, as beginners, they lost courage, or that lodgers came in and defeated their intentions, they failed that night in effecting their object. The unconscious woman was lifted into a bed, where she lay till the morning. A severe sickness was the consequence of the importunities of her new-made friends; and the colleagues, exasperated by their defeat of the previous night, were alongside of the bed, with offerings of sympathy, and more drink. In the midst of all this, she cried that she wished to get home to her beloved daughter, at the very time that she weakly accepted that which incapacitated her. By and by, the lodgers for the night began to leave the house; and the victim being once more reduced to unconsciousness, they fell to their work in the precise manner they had planned. Hare laid hold of the apertures of breathing, and Burke throwing himself on her body to repress struggles and keep down the ribs, maintained his position till the last sob escaped from the oppressed lungs; and the woman, after a struggle of fully a quarter of an hour, was a corpse. In the evening the body was conveyed to Surgeon's Square, and ten pounds procured for it.

All this tragedy was being acted while the daughter, at Gilmerton, was waiting anxiously for the return of her mother. The evening had passed without exciting in her much alarm; but when the morning came, with no mother, and no intelligence, she became oppressed with fears. Without having tasted breakfast, she sallied forth. The village was gone through, and afforded no trace. She next directed her steps to Edinburgh, inquiring at every one she met if they had seen a woman of the appearance she described. At length she resorted to the house of the gentleman who paid the pension, but beyond the information that she had been there on the previous day, she could get no satisfaction. She then wandered through all parts of the city, calling on every one she knew, and putting the same question—if they had seen her mother?—but always receiving the same answer. No weariness oppressed her in this vain search. The night set in only as a prelude to the revival of her hopes in the morning; and search followed search, and day followed day, every hour diminishing hope. The time was now counted by weeks, and as these sped, by months, yet ever as the time flew, and the hope decayed, the love increased with every accession of her grief. At length even hope was relinquished, and all speculations were lost in mystery. The only conclusion that could rationally be come to was, that the missing one had wandered by the canal and been drowned; for that a human being could disappear and be for ever lost in the city of Edinburgh, with its humane inhabitants ready to render succour, and its vigilant police ever on the watch, was what no one could conceive. The explanation was to come at a time which, to grief, might be thought long in the future; and such an explanation to a daughter! ay, and a daughter of whom the mother was so proud and so fond.

THE MOTHER
AND DAUGHTER

If we were to estimate the benefits derived from sacrificing to mammon, according to the material uses to which they are devoted, we would be apt to form a very humble estimate of his godship; but these, we suspect, constitute, even with the lowest of his worshippers, only a small part of the charm of his gifts. Seventeen pounds ten shillings, the price of one dead body, and that of the life and the corpse of another, produced a change in the economy of Log's house and in the minds of its ruling inhabitants. This appeared first in the dresses of the women, who, from being little better than trulls, with clothes bought in pawnshops, and often not far removed from ragged tanterwallops, began to be equipped like respectable people. Bonnets were got from the milliner direct; and it is even said that fine prints appeared in gaudy colours on the two women of Log's house. It was observed, too, that they held their heads higher, and walked more circumspectly, as if some species of pride—the kind we leave to the moral analyst—had asserted its universal power, undismayed by the scowl of vice. Lodgers began to be less cared for, as mere lodgers, though the most squalid of them had recommendations of another kind, of which they themselves were not aware; and as for the men, the producers of this wonderful change, they were now gentlemen at large—the huckster's cart, the hurley, the old horse, the stool, and the awl-box, having been discharged and despised as unworthy of those who held in their hands a charm invested with even greater power than the ring of Giges or Mongogul, even that of turning, by a touch, the mortal part of human nature into gold.

Hitherto even the philosophers had been wrong in their estimate of man and the world on which he lives. The ill-natured cynics represented that, in his earthly aspect, man is a parasite on the great animal the world; preying on his fellow-creatures, he is, in return, preyed upon by parasites. There are those that prey upon his body, others that, in the form of pains, ride upon the back of his vicious pleasures. There are those that fawn upon him, and feed upon his fortunes, and when he dies he is eaten by parasites. But there was in reserve, and unknown to these detractors, a chapter on human nature only laid open to our time and country, for though the Easterns had their fable of the gouls, it was received only as a fairy tale by the Westerns, till they were surprised into a belief even transcending the images of Arabian fancy. Yet the more hopeful philosophers, who draw their inspirations from Calvary, where was seen the consideration for the shekels of silver, are not dismayed. Yea, in this lowly thing we call our body, which preys on garbage, and is preyed upon in return, is a microcosm, which represents, in extension, that which has no limit—in perfection, that which is without end—in beauty, that which the poet cannot, with all his inspiration, describe.

We would not be true to human nature if we limited the effects of this change in the fortunes of Log's house to what we have already described. The vicious heart pants for pleasures to worry it. *La lampe inextinguible du plaisir* must burn, though fed with rancid oil extracted from decayed organisms; and so there was a growing increase, not only in the number, but in the intensity of the "enjoyments" of the bacchanalian nights. If the neighbours had noticed the external changes, they were not the less observant—though destined to be long ignorant of the cause—of what was nightly acted within. The brawls and fights were louder and more frequent, and the dithyrambics which mixed with them in grotesque inconsistency had more of the *ménad* of the priests of Cybele. Yet all this, by God's law, was sternly a necessity: we need no moral here. Secrecy and publicity are separate instruments of divine retribution, working strangely and mysteriously to the same end. Even the ordinary secret sin corrodes the heart by its immurement, and the sin of Log's house was not an ordinary one. The more it is suppressed, the greater the elasticity of the torment. When freed from the prison of the heart it produces that recoil of the good which isolates the criminal from the smiles of fellowship and the help of society. Yes, this is the point with the diverging paths of ruin or redemption, and Heaven still vindicates the old economy. If the sinner will be saved by penitence, he must give signs of his suffering, and the world will profit by it as well as himself. If he hurries to ruin, he will still give evidence of his agony. In either case, that Providence which watches over us will still serve its purpose.

Only one of these paths was here open, and the quaternity even rushed into it. The progress of the ruin must keep apace. The excitement, in the shape, to them, of pleasure, must be sustained; and above all, the men had tasted the *power* of money—not to be estimated by what it produced—in what simply pleased such strange natures. They had got their heads into the dagon temple, and though all the rest of the body was exposed, they felt, however much they were in danger of justice, that they had some security against a continuance of the misery and contempt of their prior lives. They must, accordingly, go on, for they were dipsomaniacs in blood. The £17, 10s. must, if it had not already, come to an end, under the expense of these nightly orgies, and, behold the prowler again out to look for a new victim.

There had been known to both of the men, and not less to the women, an unfortunate creature of the name of Mary Haldane, whose vagrant beat was the old scene of the Grassmarket. Her life had not been all through a succession of those scenes in which her class figure; for, previous to the birth of a natural child, the fruit of seduction, she had been not only respected for a fair reputation, but looked on favourably for those personal qualities so often the means of ruin. Then the demon drink had met her at that turn of the fortunes of so many of her kind, when decayed beauty is not compensated by the consolations of penitence. The road down was easy, even to that stage where flapping rags could scarcely cover the body. Need we say that this creature was likely, when the prowler knew from his own experience that she would drink *to the point*. One day he accordingly issued forth to seek for Mary, but Mary had been in the drink fever for days, and he could only regret that so favourable a condition had not ensued in Log's house, where the termination would not have been the recovery which this time once more awaited her. Exasperated by his disappointment, he was only the more determined to overlook other tempting objects in that fruitful field of human weeds, fit enough for death's scythe. Nor had he to wait long. Two days afterwards Mary was standing at the mouth of the narrow close up which she lived.[6] The moment he saw her, the old smile and eloquent twinkle again illuminated or darkened his face, for he was as sure of his prey as the fox is of its spoil when it sits in the roost with its head under its wing. Nor was the smile less expressive that Mary presented to him. The red and swollen eyes, the quivering cheeks, and all the other signs of that unhappiness through which the rebel spirit will still shoot its buoyance in spite of depressed nature. Misery is easily approached. The dram is again the bribe, and the kindliness of the offer a recommendation, which was as much a surprise as a pleasure to one from whom all kindliness had been long barred by the magnetic repulsion of poverty and degradation. Poor Mary was once more happy; and, accompanying her "friend," she trudged along to the place where the *envied* stimulant awaited her.

As they were slowly wending their way along the West Port, the people, as some of them afterwards stated, looked earnestly at the couple, without being able to explain the sympathy which brought them together; for already Hare was upon the rise in society, with a new coat and hat, and even a tie; but the presence of the *gentleman* did not prevent the children from pursuing their old game of teazing Mary, nor could the threatenings of her protector keep them off. At this juncture, who should approach from the opposite direction but the colleague. The mutual smile—yea, more. Would Burke, who had the character of being serviceable to the unfortunate, permit Mary Haldane to be abused while he was present? He would protect the friendless; and so the boys got a drubbing, and injured misfortune was vindicated. Having accomplished this act of justice, Burke, who had now so little to do, and was so far above cobbling, proceeded on what had been intended as a pleasant stroll, while his friend and Mary held their way to Log's lodgings. In a short time he was seen to return with a quicker step; and by and by they are all assembled in the little dark room "with the window looking out on the dead wall"—where the women, who knew that the money was getting exhausted, received them with their peculiar welcome.

Well, you expect something, and already the heart throbs,— and do not stop it; for pity does not close her eye upon the unfortunate, even where sin has contributed to the misery of the sufferer. But here you cannot help yourself: the inevitable recoil from cruelty will open the issues of compassion whether you will or no; and so strangely formed are we, that here you may be the more willing to acknowledge the soft emotion, that Mary's eyes reeled with delight when she saw Helen M'Dougal place upon the table a supply of whisky, which to her share would transcend even the necessities of "the want" after the fever. There was on this occasion no necessity for the siren song to charm into confidence where the bottle was, a band more hallowed, in the estimation of the guest, than the pledges of love. Neither Hare's sardonic jollity nor Burke's pathos was needed where the work was apparently so easy; and they were no longer neophytes, but adepts, not only in confidence, but manipulation. Yea, it was the work of apprentices, and they were journeymen; nor was it necessary that they should concern themselves with more than filling the glass and contemplating the imbodied value—ten pounds—as, by her fading energies and impending unconsciousness, it assumed its full proportions. All is ready— the drooping head—the closing eye—the languid, helpless body. The women get the hint. They knew the unseemliness of being spectators—nay, they were delicate. A repetition of the former scene, only with even less resistance. Hare holds again the lips, and Burke presses his twelve stone weight. Scarcely a sigh; but on a trial if dead, a long gurgling indraught. More required— and all is still in that dark room "with the window looking out on the dead wall."

After a preliminary visit to the College, where arrangement was made for the reception, the colleagues carried their burden, at an hour approaching to twelve, to its destination. As usual, it was examined before payment,—the amount of which, in this instance, we do not know; but, whether from some want of success, consequent on the increased watchfulness over cemeteries, attending the midnight adventures of our friends Merrylees and the "Spune," or from a greater avidity for science on the part of the surgeons, it is certain that, as the supply from Log's lodgings increased, the value given for a burden became greater, amounting, in some instances, to £12 or £14.

The band was thus again supplied with resources, and the consequence was an increase of extravagance and riot—the former exhibiting itself in a still more inconsistent style of dress on the part of the females, and the latter in more frequent disturbances of the neighbours. Even questions began to be put to Helen M'Dougal, which were parried by the intelligence that she communicated,—that she had fallen heir to some house property about her place of birth, and that it was only right that decent people should rise in the world, and take the use of their own. Nor was Mary Hare less adroit in her fences. But the explanations thus given of what appeared to be a mystery were not deemed satisfactory, though no theory could be formed by the remonstrants.

On the part of the *fortunate* crew, the sums they received seemed only to stimulate their avidity. Not now waiting for the dispersion of the earnings, they aimed at a store, perhaps apprised by some looming suspicion that their fortune was too good to last, and a strange circumstance soon threw another temptation in their way. Young Mary Haldane, the daughter of her whom we have seen so easily and suddenly removed from the world and life, with all those sins on her head which had accumulated from the day of her seduction, had been brought up by the mother to ways as shameless as her own. As yet, however, it was the morning of life to the girl, and it is not always or often that wayward affections spent upon men more profligate than themselves, diminish the love of such creatures to their parents, even if the latter ought, by their neglect, to have earned nothing but hatred. We have seen one daughter cast into inconsolable grief, another was to be a wanderer and inquirer for her parent, with another and even more terrible issue. Having ascertained, on the morning subsequent to that evening when the burden was conveyed to Surgeon's Square, that her mother had not been seen on the previous night, Mary occupied the day in searching. The woman was a ken-speckle, the familiar object of all in the neighbourhood, as well as the game of the urchins; and much curiosity was added to the sympathy for the orphan, who, unfortunately, was scarcely less notorious. Many aided in the inquiry, but with no more success, of course, than that which attended the efforts of the daughter. It is still remembered how she went about in her decayed finery, with swollen eyes, and the tears on her cheeks, sobbing out her grief, amidst the fruitless question, "Had any one seen Mary Haldane?" At length, one of the neighbours was told by a grocer in Portsburgh, that the woman had been seen going towards Log's lodgings in the company of William Hare—a trace which, as no suspicions as yet attached to the man, held out some hope of success.

The information was immediately conveyed to the young woman, who thereupon hastened to the West Port, where she got the story confirmed, with all the minutiæ of Burke's gallant rescue of Hare's *protégée* from the assaults of the urchins. Nor did she stop till she got to Log's lodgings. Mrs Hare denied that the woman had ever been in her house—a statement corroborated by Helen M'Dougal, who, in her new-born pride, resented the imputation that it could be possible for the beggar to have the impudence to approach the residence of respectable people; but Hare, who in the back room had heard the rencontre, came forth, and taking the part of the girl—with what expression of countenance to his companions, it would be difficult for a mere pen to give the symbols of an idea—sympathised with her, and even more, asked her to come into the room with the window opening to the dead wall, and get a dram to dry up her tears. The girl, also given to drink, was tempted, and complied with the kind invitation. It was not long till the colleague made his appearance, having, it is supposed, seen Mary enter when he was lounging idly about the top of the close. They were no sooner seated, and the whisky put upon the table by Helen M'Dougal, than Hare began his explanation. He told her that her mother had spoken to him on that day when she disappeared; that she told him she was going to Midcalder, (where he knew she had some friends;) and that he had no doubt she would be found there, to the great joy of the despairing girl.

And no doubt the poor girl's heart jumped to the valediction. She began to get cheerful under the new-lighted lamp of hope; and if there was any deficiency in the oil, it was supplied by the cognate combustible which, like all other agents of the same kind, consumes by its latent fires those who consume it. Glass succeeded glass, and with hope getting brighter and brighter before her eyes, now dry enough, and sympathy sounding louder and louder in her ears, what marvel that Mary Haldane should be as happy as those who had preceded her in those jubilations. She talked of her lovers and her youthful escapades—not forgetting those whisky-born fortunes, embracing equipages and servants, which are the continual destiny of the wretched, as if nature, in some mood of pity, made an imaginary compensation for real privations and as real misery. How little conscious was she that the two men, who responded so exuberantly to her wild aspirations, were watching when they would exhaust and bring her "to the point." Nor was the issue long delayed. Mary was one of those who, once fairly begun, never stopped, if the means were in her power, till she had run the full course. The symptoms of the artificial narcosis began to shew themselves,— the thick speech, the heavy eye, the bent head, and only a little longer and she was extended on the floor. Let us not speak of this girl's youth, the interest of her peculiar fortunes, with no chance ever given her of putting even the first step in the path of virtue. Why, there was, even in the estimation of those who stood over, ready for the work of their calling, a curious if not stimulating aptitude in sending her after her mother. Did she not call there to see her, and find her? and why should they defeat so laudable a purpose? The quarter of an hour's suspension between life and death, with those mysterious agonies of which the organism is capable, even in the absence of manifestations, or at least in their suppression by external force, and Mary Haldane experienced the fate of her mother. And with her mother, too, she lay that night in the hall of Surgeon's Square.

THE
GRANDMOTHER
AND THE DUMB BOY

It has been said, that in the course of one man's life there occurs usually only one springtide on which he may direct his barque to fortune, and, so far as we have seen, this chance was not denied to the governors of Log's lodgings; but nature has not equally decreed that the voyagers shall see beyond that fortune, or to what it may lead. Nay, is there not something in the circumference of the objects of a day, if not an hour, if not a minute, which, like that which surrounds the scorpion, keeps all inside inviolate from the anathemas beyond? But then the circumference is ever changing, and ever enclosing new objects, till the last, with an opening in the side, looks out upon the dark or light theatre of retribution or salvation. We sometimes see this solitary springtide surmounted by the shattered barque of age, from which the waters of life are fast receding, and yet the voyager moves on. His fortune is a *hysteria*, through the ecstatic delirium of which he cannot see the gulf before his nose. These two men and two women whose history we record were on their springtide, and we are not to wonder that, beyond the circumference of rock and cloud, they were prevented from looking; not that there were not openings through which they could see ruin, but that the insanity of a fruitful wickedness made them revel blindly in the buoyancy of their progress, heedless of all rocks and gulfs of retribution.

Poor moralising this, we suspect, as regards men whose pleasures, bought at such a price of a revolt against nature, could be termed only "painted pain." But even they could not be exempted from the laws of human nature. The circle behoved to contain its objects, and to change from day to day till the last came, with the lateral opening looking into perdition; perhaps any other mode ever devised by man of bringing sacrifices to mammon might not have been utterly exclusive of an attempt to get into a caste above. Bankrupts, thieves, adulterers, and even ordinary murderers, sometimes in our day try their hands at this, and make wonderful successes, for even these crimes which make men what they are, are not absolutely incompatible with a modern conventional status; but the crime of the men of our history involved in its very nature the impossibility of ever holding up the head in any other way than a swagger of desperation, or directing the eyes to an honest face, except as a look of dogged defiance. So, in addition to those evidences of change at Log's lodgings, we have only to mention the restlessness of the moneyed vagabonds driving them out to the streets to pull companions of their grade into drinking-houses, and treating them with the money which, however they might love it, burnt their hands that dispensed it. The delirium of intoxication amidst living objects that carried the mind out, was the refuge from, not the spectre of conscience, for conscience they had none, but that of justice, which no averting of the eyes could enable them to avoid, only the reeling of them could make it a changing phantasmagoria.

And why, when we have so much deeper tragedies to recount, ought we to stop our narrative to record—unless, indeed, for the mere sake of the arithmetic of murders—a mere interlude resorted to as a relief from dithyrambism? Childermas day came round again! Poor Joe the miller could bring his price of eleven pounds as well as the rest of them. No doubt, when he offered himself, in the heyday of his life, to Jenny the farmer's daughter, he thought himself of greater account than merely eleven pounds; but men undergo deterioration. Even when rejected, he would have spurned the valuation when he sung that jolly song of independence so often sung by his craft, and which declares the determination that neither lawyer nor doctor would "e'er get a fee from him,"—true enough, yet, alas! not false in the reverse, that doctors would give a fee *for* him. Joe's miscalculations were due to his ignorance of the effects of intemperance, for it will not do to say that these are known when every day brings up new developments of consequences resulting from this most dangerous of all the voluntary evils of man. Say that the drunkard dares the advent of poverty, crime, the horrors of *delirium tremens*—death,—could he say that this last is a greater violence to nature than that produced by the grip and the pressure which, in all these cases, were only consequent upon the inebriation, which, again, was the act of his own will? It was while in a state of inebriety that the prowler met Joe. He was already made and prepared, and the subsequent decoyment, the additional drink, the final onset of the grim actors, their success, were only the development of a drama wrought out by actors who took an advantage accorded by himself. Our authority for treating this case as a mere interlude is derived from the admission of Burke himself, who, as a great judge could estimate the importance of what by others cannot be estimated at all, for the simple reason that the smallest of these tragedies so far transcends all power of comprehension that comparison becomes a farce; yet though this once jolly son of a jolly craft might have earned the contempt attributed to a facility of dying, he was, we are assured, mourned in the hamlet of his birth, where his frailties, if condemned, were placed, as is too often the case, to the account of a good heart. Nay, for aught we know,—and we say it the more readily that no one can trace or enumerate the threads which the poorest of God's creatures leaves ramifying from heart to heart, all to respond, as by electric sympathy, to the shock of his death,—the farmer's daughter might even be concussed to tears—how much too late—when the terrible tragedy was divulged. We may be at least certain that Joe never dreamed that a man's character in the world depends upon his manner of leaving it, or he would have saved his reputation by a greater resistance when the enemies were upon him, but he was also then too late: the devil, whom he might have fought with and defeated if sober, had taken on a strange form, and was unknown to the victim, for the reason that the victim did not know himself.

However unimportant he might be in these annals, the price which the miller brought was sufficient to stimulate the now, and long before, irredeemable actors to a deed which, in the estimation of Burke himself, as it must ever be in that of a blushing nation, stood unparalleled among his own atrocities, as by all experiences else it was unparalleled in the world. Before entering upon the detail, we feel inclined to philosophise a little. We have been obliged to speak of these men as men, because they possessed all the physical characters of the species. In a natural view it has been said that, by the presence of the lower animals in the world, man is more injured in his ideas of a high nature and destiny than he is benefited in the temporal advantages of being fed and clothed by them. The Roman felt the inconveniences of the presence of apes in the same world with him, when he cried out, in rage or satire or pity, *Simia, quam similis, turpissima bestia, nobis!* Then what is the use of these beings always putting us in mind of our resemblance to them? If we are to believe Pythagoras, Mr Tweddel, or Mr Smith, or any one of the vegetarians, we could, in their absence, live on herbs and fruits, and be clothed with cotton and linen. Their presence in the same world, and with so much in common with us, is a continual satire on man's psychological privilege or peculium, and to get quit of this many early nations accorded a soul and a hereafter to them. The satire was inverted when men made gods of them. We of a modern age shew our respect by an act of parliament against being cruel to them; and secondly, by eating them. In the midst of such curious speculations we are always apt to forget that within the moralities of our species we have gorillas far fiercer than any brother or sister of that "splendid specimen" described by Du Chaillu, and yet the strength and savagery of this animal have been called in doubt.

One day, about a month after the disposal of Joe the miller, Hare was again on the track of the unfortunate, and this time, as it was said, sent out by his colleague, as if the latter had wished to seek in repetition the assuagement of familiarity. Alas! the old search. You cry me mercy, and I would forbear did I not know that truth must bear her crown amidst the lying conventionalities of refinement; and virtue, who is her companion, looks to her for strength, while she shines the brighter for the proximity of vice. Yes, the old threading through the mazes of human beings,—now passing between the ripe and the raw, the full-blooded youth and the tottering beggar, the rich and the poor— apportioning the meed of his approbation according to the selective affinities of the possible. Polypheme had no tastes; this man was refined. Yea, even like the good philanthropist who passes by those who do not require his help, and turns kindly to the maimed and the blind and the miserable, his were claimed by those on whom the hard and heavy hand of calamity had pressed. The goddess pitied Iphigenia, and made her a priestess, not because she was beautiful and the daughter of a great king, but because she was unfortunate.

But on this occasion the searcher was *sought*. While standing on the High Street holding the button of the ragged coat of an old man who pleased him, and whose escape, seeing he was a dipsomaniac, would be nothing short of miracle, there came up to him an Irishwoman, also advanced in years, apparently a weary tramp, her shoes covered with dust, and her poor clothes looking as if she had slept in them all night among straw. She was a stranger in a strange city, and by her side was a little boy whom she held by the hand, for he was one of God's stricken— deaf and dumb—with that wistful peering of the eyes which is as often the effect of the infirmity as of the habit of solicitation. She told him that she was from Ireland, that she was on the search for some one of her countrymen or countrywomen whom she knew, and from whom she intended to claim that privilege of friendship and assistance which the people of that country, with all their faults, are so liberal in according. Was there need for a bond of confidence? He himself was of the ould country, and would he not assist a country-woman with a charge so helpless, so pitiful, so burdensome, except for the love which bore it? Nay, did he not know the very person she sought? and did she not reside in Log's lodgings, whereto he would be so delighted to lead her? Happy escape for the button-held, and yet strange freak of the mind as it works awry often for an opposite; for he seemed, as he departed, to envy the new comer, who had thus secured the friendship of one now possessed of money, and not backward in shewing it.

So along they went, up between the high houses of Edinburgh's principal thoroughfare and down by the then Old Bow, with its strange old fronts and leering storm windows, as if they were curious about the modern people, so unlike their ancient inhabitants, all which sights raised a wonderment in the western Celt, which could only be satisfied by questions, and which, again, were answered with as much particularity as if she was not only to see them all again, but to seek them out for a purpose. Then how the boy watched the face of the man, as if some instinct had told him he would befriend his grandmother, and be in the room of a father to him. And what had this boy ever learned yet through his eyes alone, to be able to read backwards the looks of love. Do we not get dreary? The road has no windings, and there are no trees to conceal the cave of skulls on the Aventinian mount. Once again with his victim,—for surely we cannot count the deaf and dumb boy with the wistful eyes as being destined to have his name—if it could be known in the strange country—recorded in the list, within the little back room. The colleague was there, lying drowsy from the prior night's potations, but not unexpectant of the return of his friend. His eye brightened as the quickened orb threw off the drowsy vapours; and could he be otherwise than polite—the word is not misapplied—to the strangers? But where was the Irish friend? Oh, she would come in good time; and though it were long, did not Helen M'Dougal place upon the table, in a goodly bottle, that which qualified the ardour of impatience? The boy must be cared for too till the friend came, and Mary Hare would do that duty in the front room—yea, might there not have been sweetmeats in Log's lodgings when the Logs had now waxed wealthy? In two hours that woman was lying a corpse in the bed of the small room "with the window looking out on the dead wall." The boy was dumb, but he had wistful eyes, and begged imploringly with these to see his grandmother. The women could not even lie to him, and tell him he would see her in the morning.

In the evening the two men sat over the fire in that same room, with the body of the woman stretched out on the bed which was at the back of the wall behind them. The boy was still under the charge of Mary Hare in the front room. Every moment that had separated him from his grandmother—to him all the world of his knowledge and affections—rendered the duty of the governess more difficult, and even strange sounds, between a groan and a scream, made their way out of his speechless mouth, as if nature in an agony struggled against her own decrees. The sounds found their way to the back room, and it came to be a question with the men, as they still sat looking into the fire, what was to be done with him. It was proposed by one, we know not which, that he should be taken out in the dark to the Canongate and there left. The policy had two reasons to support it. In the first place, he could not peach, and was therefore safe; in the second, they could hardly venture the offer of two burdens, however welcome at Surgeon's Square, for fear of awakening suspicions, a reason, this latter, which was rejected by the other, supposed to be Burke, for the other reason, that the boy, when dead, could be kept in the house for a few days without great depreciation in value; and even if they should get for him a pound or two less, they could make it up upon a fresher one next time.

There was thus some little disagreement between the faithful friends, which must await a settlement; and, in the meantime, Hare went out to get a tea-chest for the conveyance of the inhabitant of the bed against the wall. On his departure, his friend sat ruminating. At one time, when alone, and amidst the sombre yet sometimes *soft* influences of melancholy, with her throng of shades of the past and gone, he used to sing to himself plaintive airs. Perhaps his melancholy at these times was poetical. These shades point to the ghosts of our friends, that seem to stand on yonder shore of the land of shadows, and beckon us to them. We resist the appeal from day to day for the sake of those that remain. These die too, and the crowd of beckoners increases, till all that formed our world seem to have flitted away, and then we make the sign of resignation to the hermit shadow (in his case the hangman) that is to lead us to them. If he ever did indulge in these plaintive airs, now was the propitious time, but his mind was engaged on something more practical—the resolution, turned and turned again, and examined and laid aside to come back—yes, the resolution to send the boy after his grandmother.

The night passed, the boy having by some means been made to understand that his protectress was in bed unwell, but the mutterings of the mute might have indicated that he had fears which, perhaps, he could not comprehend. The morning found the resolution of the prior night unshaken; and, in that same back room where the grandmother lay, Burke took the boy on his knee, and, as he himself expressed it, broke his back. No wonder that he described this scene as the one that lay most heavily upon his heart, and said that he was haunted by the recollection of the piteous expression of the wistful eyes as the victim looked in his face. The lad was laid on the bed along with his grandmother; and in the evening an old herring barrel held the couple who in life were each to each the one thing loved— and love is the same in the high and the low—had the same fate, enclosed in the same receptacle, and dealt with in the same way in Surgeon's Square.

It was recorded that a curious incident happened in connexion with this affair which had wellnigh put a stop to the career of these wonderful men, and we cannot help thinking, in looking back upon it, that it should not have led to a complete discovery. The herring barrel, containing the two bodies, was placed in a cart. An old horse, which Hare had used in his traffic in fish and crockery-ware, was yoked to it, and the two set out in the darkening to Surgeon's Square with their cargo. They proceeded along the West Port without anything remarkable happening, but when they reached the marketplace, at the entrance to the Grassmarket, the horse stopped, and, notwithstanding all their efforts, would not move a leg. They were in confusion. Exposure was imminent. As Burke afterwards said, they thought "the poor old horse had risen up in judgment against them." A crowd collected, but, strangely enough, the people were so much occupied with the horse that they never thought of inquiring what was in the cart; and when it was found that neither entreaties nor blows would induce the animal to move forward, two porters were allowed to bear off the burden without any particular notice. Nay, these men so much less squeamish than the horse, took the barrel to the dissecting rooms without ever asking what they were carrying. The horse, which it is probable age and hard usage had arrested in its progress, was, in revenge for the fright it had caused its masters, led to a neighbouring tannery and slaughtered. It was of no value in Surgeon's Square.[7]

THE STRAY WAIFS

There is no great wonder that thinking people, while admitting ruling motives of action, should be chary about the question of their origin; how one rises out of another, and that out of one further removed, and so forth, as deep down as you please. The harlequin jackets may be removed one after another, till you come to the skin, which, being white, is said to be of no colour, only a negative, as also has been said of black. In another view, the subject appears still more unfruitful; for, as you may bring a tune, combining the grave and the gay, out of one length of catgut, so the human mind will give you off all sorts of feelings, some good and some bad, in the course of the same hour. In truth, as our doings are made up of passions and restraints, which latter may be passions as well, we will never understand thoroughly a human action. When we admit that these great criminals took away lives, right and left, for the sake of money, how much do we achieve? We just accuse them of what the Greeks called *chrysomania*, or madness for gold. Strange that in our country, where the passion is pretty strong, we have no such name, avarice being entirely different; but this passion may have been a rider on the love of drink, and then we cannot estimate either the one or the other, till we know the force of the countervailing restraints. If these—and there are many—are weak or *nil*, the passion may be a very weak affair, so that such beings as our principal actors might—seeing they wanted pity and religion and fear—have thought less of suffocating a fellow-creature than Bellarmine did of removing a fly from his face. With no pretension to be teachers, we offer these hints merely as explanatory of our manner of treating a subject much discussed at the time.

Of one thing, however, we may be certain, and that is, the effect of familiarity in removing those inconvenient asperities called scruples, which nature is continually casting up to preserve the triumph of the good over the evil; and so we may well be satisfied that every succeeding success operated with the double effect of confirming the prior purpose and stimulating to a repetition. This is merely the confidence inspired by habit, with which we are all daily cognisant; and therefore the subsequent atrocities ought really to excite less curiosity, though not less revulsion, than those that went before. Yet this is not found to be the case, and the reason is, that even great men in the murdering way are generally content with one trial, as being sufficient for all their power to carry before the judgment-seat of God.

It is always to be remembered that all these moral wonders took place in very quick succession, and only a few weeks pass until we arrive at the waifs. The actors had come to see that they had a great stage to perform on, and supplied as well with innumerable objects. They had only to look a few yards to the west, up Portsburgh, or to the east, up the Grassmarket and Cowgate, to be certain that "a ten pounds," all prepared, was walking or staggering as if every roll to a side offered to be one into their arms. They had thus reason, if they had been of a philosophical habit,—and one had the poetry of sentiment— to thank the great genius Society for his injustice to his own members. And what an extraordinary injustice it appears, when we consider that the high head of Wealth is upheld by the tax of respect imposed upon the poor and the humble! If there were no inferiors to witness a man's greatness, he would be great no more; and yet those who are the soil from which this moral grandness springs are left to rot, as if the more it approached to compost the ranker would be the tribute to his mightiness: so, without abating our horror of these men, we cannot altogether forget that the sufferers in most instances were cast away by Mammon to be in turn immolated to Mammon.

They had in short a bank—Heaven knows, not of "elegance"—

upon which they could pass a draft when they chose; nor was it forged—they were themselves the drawers, and the money seemed to belong to no one; so careless at that time—it is, we hope, different now—was society of those whom it was bound to look after and protect. So money was again needed, and Burke was to pass the draft, because perhaps his companion thought that as there is (of course) honour among thieves, so fair play must be esteemed a jewel among manslayers. And here the strange circumstance occurred, in the midst of all these strange things, that his draft was to be endorsed *by a constable*. He had been among his dear friends in the Canongate,—and a man or a woman had now a value for him which a short time before he never dreamt of,—thinking of how he could make some of them more dear to him than they seemed to be to themselves, when his attention was directed to a poor unfortunate, steeped in poverty and drink, in the hands of a police officer. Mixing with the crowd, he went up to the officer, and, with much apparent sympathy, interfered for one who had no home and no friends to care for her. He would furnish that home, at least for a time, and be that friend. The poor woman, like some of the others who had wondered that they should become objects of interest, looked at him as one may be supposed to do who has considered herself past the hope of man's charity. Some of the crowd, struck with the offer, backed the sympathiser, and the policeman, considering for a little, at last consented, giving her up to the kind friend,—no other than a philanthropist of the humbler order, but perhaps not the less sincere,—and enjoining upon him the due performance of his promise.

Having got his charge, the crowd—whose curiosity was served not less than its benevolence, for these poor people feel intensely for each other's sorrows, the more by reason that no one else does—separated. Then, alas! the old story. The tempter and the victim pace the streets towards the block-altar of the sacrifice; and as they go, we may consider how many have achieved a world-wide notoriety for having concocted one of these acts, with the attending circumstances of having watched their opportunity and been defeated, and still kept to their purpose, and, veiling all in romantic mystery, at length effected their object. Such men, and their solitary performance, with which they were contented, or to which they were limited by the gallows, are only qualified to form a meagre episode to the terrible drama we are with so much imperfection evolving; even as Faust's vision rose in curling smoke, and took on the gigantic form of a being out of nature and belonging to another world. We have heard of hardened men who gave those they intended to sacrifice time to pray. There was allowed only short shrift in Log's lodgings. Before nightfall this woman lay doubled up in a tea-chest. We will not disturb you in your pause as your mind, led by her who dropped pity's tear on the written words of the recording angel, goes away back to the youth or the maidenhood of this woman. The "perhaps" has a weakness in it, but who shall gainsay, with the doctrine of chances against him, that she was, as you may be, beautiful and good, yea, at one time looking forward to years of happiness, a redeemed's death, and a Christian's funeral, even with that confidence which—blessings on your pitiful heart!—will be sanctified and verified to you, because it is in God?

We are not done with the waifs even so far as known, and their number has never been recorded. It was a practice of Burke to wander out in the early mornings. He would have been seen pacing the solitude of the deserted streets even before cock-crow. Nor could any man tell the reason: it was not asked, not even speculated upon. Like the traces of sympathetic ink, the notice lay unverified, till the great disclosure, when it came up fresh into many minds. And it came up all at once, with the suspicion that he did not go those solitary rounds for contemplation, far less from remorse; a feeling which, so far as can be ascertained—for the pang of the wistful look of the dumb boy was suspected to be a mere trick of the prison confessional—never ruffled his pillow. The night-hawk goes to bed in the early morning, before the choir offer their song to the rising sun, and these catch no flies till he is far up in the heavens. The first surmise of the discovery of what had been doing in Log's lodgings sprang the suspicion with elastic rapidity, that these early walks were undertaken in prosecution of the old purpose, and specially stimulated by an interest in that institution—to be found, we believe, nowhere else—the cinder-women;[8] not singing-birds these, if he was not a night-hawk; but the osprey is as early on the long sands, when there is not to be seen there a living thing, except the gulls, as they pace so securely the edge of the sea.

A very early riser in Edinburgh is impressed with the sight of these thin, haggard figures flitting from backet to backet in the great solitude. The only moving creatures in the long streets,—if you did not know they had any other object in view,—you would think that, being immured in the dark dens of the Old Town, and ashamed to shew their faces during the day, they crawl out to get a *glimpse* of their old haunts, where, as unfortunates, (the greater number,) they once flaunted their charms, till they faded to the point of recoil. You would say, too, that they belonged neither to this world nor any other—mere pendencies, with no solidity to keep them on the earth, and no wings to take them from it—hopeless, too, and fearless, not from despair or passion, but from sheer inanity—glimmers, not lights, flickering at the end of wicks, with no oil except what they have imbibed long before. It was this prey that brought the prowler out so early in the morning; and he might have revelled in a field so fruitful long enough, without that risk of discovery which attended his other assaults. Friendless as they are, with years intervening since they were cast off, not only from society, but from those who once knew them,—some worshippers of beauty, perhaps,— there were none to inquire after them, scarcely any to miss them, except a sister straggler, who might wonder for a moment why a shadow had disappeared.

That more of these creatures fell into his hands than the culprit confessed, was the general opinion of the time. One, at least, was certain, as a waif scarcely worthy of mention among so many cases, and these so much more *éclatants*. On that eventful morning he was more early than usual; the gray mists only as yet disappearing, and the figures he sought for looming as shadows here and there at long intervals. It was supposed to be in the New Town where he encountered the hopeless, soulless creature, scraping as usual in a dust-box, picking up the bits of cinders, and peering in the dim light for the chance turn-up of the sign of some servant's *lâcheté*. A more easy approach than ever, with the charmed "dram" on his lips, sufficient to bring the light of hope once more to the cinder eyes. Even the long distance from the New Town, by the Mound and the Bow, to Log's lodgings, as they paced and paced, would only increase the hope, to be gratified at the end. And of course it was gratified; so cheap a purchase, too, where the oil was all in the wick, and the blue glimmer, rendered for a short time white by a glass only once repeated, would recede into unconsciousness almost before the energy to take advantage of it was up in arms. While this work was doing, in which the accomplice rose from his sleep to join, the women were in bed—saved in this instance from the trouble of their delicacy in going into another room, or the passage, as they sometimes did. Nay, the cock had not crowed before all was over. The gurgling sound would be weak. It has been said that the death-scream of the surprised sinner, and the dying prayer of the Christian, are the extremes which terminate two courses of life. They may be the last signs in this world and the first in the next, as they are the farewell to time or the salutation to eternity. Who was there to care?

THE RELATIVE

So far we have had details through the medium of confessions uttered when the only *terriculumentum* to be feared by those who had no belief in a hereafter—the law—had given forth her decree of death, supplemented as these were by collateral testimony, or, rather, desultory remarks of others who had seen portions of the drama; but in some instances there were thrown across the light which at last illuminated the mystery, certain shadows with no defined forms, and through which the light shone only to make them lurid.

Of this kind of partially-revealed secrets was the story of the young cousin. No name or personal marks or place of origin ever came to the public ear, far less the form or features of the sacrificed; only, and no more, that a cousin of Helen M'Dougal's,—by uncle or aunt uncertain,—left her mother and sister,—from whence, also under the gnome,—to visit her relative in Edinburgh. It was known that she entered under the door-lintel of Log's lodgings, and was never seen again. If the world, as a spasmodic poet tells us, were destroyed, a few atoms left of the wreck, with their internal forces of attraction and repulsion, would enable a philosopher to tell how it was made. We smile at the extravagance, while we acknowledge some kind of truth, which we cannot understand. These small traces of the little world of crime within the back room "with the window looking out on the dead wall," long since destroyed and erased from the bigger world of which it formed a part and the shame, may be brought together and filled up by the imagination, with a certainty so far removed from the feeling of fiction, that we might scarcely regret the want of particulars. We have had small need of that faculty in our history; yet, comparatively, of that

little world we know next to nothing. We might as well deny
to the welcomed cousin a name and a place of birth, as refuse
to believe that she went into that house with the expectation of
meeting friendship, if not love, to a greater degree than what
was held out to the hope of others. They would shake hands with
her—(what love and hypocrisy don't?)—and there would be
inquiries after the mother, and the sister too;—just what takes
place at all such meetings. Nor are we to forget the welcome in
the still more common shape, not the fatted calf, but the bottle
of whisky, so useful an auxiliary there. If the paramour or
husband of her cousin ever sung his sentimental airs, he would
surely not refuse on the occasion of a visit of one allied to him
in the bonds of affinity. There could not help being joy, for it was
through the light of the feeling of mirth that these eight eyes
looked on the guest they were making happy. Those who have
read the German tale of the two eyes which followed everywhere
Hans Kauffmann, and never glared upon him but when he was
alone in the dark, and which at an after-period he saw shining in
the face of his enemy, as that enemy, the wreaker of vengeance,
stood over him with the thirsty sword, may trace a resemblance;
but as for these eyes of the four hosts looking anger on the poor
relative, we may safely place that among the impossibilities—and
surely we do that more easily than we can fancy the expression
of that peculiar welcome.

We wonder how nature so often leaves us in the dark. We
cannot understand that she has so much to do that she is for
ever in a hurry, so that we only see at times the skirt of her cloak.
Then we are ourselves so restless and impatient for knowledge,
that we snuff the candle of our inquiry so often that we can see
nothing. Perhaps all this is intended for the purpose of giving
us a wider world of imagination, and more ardour in peopling
it with all its strange beings, spectral images, protean forms,
wild movements—for what further end we know not, but we
work our privilege in these days of fiction very well. The veil
is often an exaggerator, but in this act of our drama it seems

hard to fill up the unknown recesses with possibilities equal to the realities. Just try to supply the required minutiæ to the few words said to have been uttered by Helen M'Dougal. After many months of fruitless inquiry, met with a denial that any one in Log's lodgings had seen the young cousin, the mother and sister, probably under suspicion of some foul play, went to the house of Constantine Burke, the brother of our man. Helen M'Dougal happened to be present, and to the request again made to know what had become of the girl, the woman, who must have been under the influence of drink, for at this time the explosion had not taken place, answered, "Oh, you need not trouble yourselves about Jessy. She was murdered, and sold long ago."

Among the cases of mere outline and shadowy traces, suspected to have been more in number, as including more waifs than admitted, we may place another. It seems to have been a bargain between the two principal actors that their work should be conjunct in action as well as in payment. On one occasion, Burke, having now plenty of money, went to the country on a pleasure jaunt. Yes; pleasure. Amidst all our philosophy and inquiry into causes and motives, would we not save ourselves a deal of trouble by attributing nine-tenths of the actions of men, not excepting murder, to a desire for pleasure? All swallow the love-apple bait presented by some wicked genius of the devil, who sports with the affections of mankind. The beguiler laughs as he angles. Some victims afford him fine "rises," and look shy, only to come again to bite in earnest. Some swallow and enjoy the sweet morsel, until the hook approaches the pylorus of their reason. Some disgorge it, to seek it again; others break the line and run away with the hook, to die in secret places under a crag. Some are caught by a fin, and carry the mark of the forbidden pleasure only to excite them to another trial; others are held on till they reach the bank, where they writhe in agony amidst sunbeams, wild thyme, and gaudy flowers, with the laugh of the tempter sounding in their ears. And some, on being swung ashore, get entangled *in a tree*, and hang there by the neck. How few can nibble off cunningly the *cibum præfixum ære*, and avoid the snare! Burke had gone on a pleasure jaunt—not to be hooked yet. On his return he found Log's lodgings as he left them; nor did he suspect that any of the unholy work had been performed in his absence. If the old orgies had been continued,—and how could they now be renounced when the increasing weight of all those deeds must have been pressing more and more on their hearts, however they might try to conceal it, and required the old art of buoyancy as a counter-agent?—there had been plenty of money to supply the means, so that Burke thought that no march had been stolen upon him by his cunning colleague. It happened, however, that he had occasion soon after his return to call at the hall in Surgeon's Square—perhaps to get the price, or part of it, of the last burden. He was there told by one of the assistants that his friend had been there shortly before with a box, not empty, and had been paid for it. He even got the day of the month and the hour of the evening, from which he saw that his co-actor had been secretly, as he said, working during his absence "on his own hook." Enraged at this want of honour, he repaired to the house, where he found his friend, and taxed him with the fraud. Hare stoutly denied the charge. The women were appealed to, but neither of them would admit anything; for we are to remember that both of them were not only in fear of their respective lords, but of those of each other. Nay, we have seen Hare using as much liberty of punishing M'Dougal when his friend was present, as Burke had of thrashing Mrs Hare, which it is certain he often did. Nay, the women even had their battles royal, and the men were, as well, often engaged in fierce conflict. The present subject was a *delicate* one. It touched the honour of contractors, the purse of sordidness, and the faith of friendship. Well, we verily believe that even Burke was fit for these heroics, and he was fit for something else. He fell upon his friend with fury, and Hare, ever ready for battle with all and sundry, not excepting his wife, retaliated. They fought long and desperately, the women looking on with only that concern which might find its account in so being revenged for some prior cruelty exercised toward them by one or the other, perhaps both. This was one of those riots which so much disturbed the neighbours. A crowd, as usual, collected at the door, but even the exasperation of the parties could not force out the secret of their quarrel. It would have been strange indeed if it had! and we say this even in the midst of daily examples of anger roused to a pitch of opening the floodgates of very dark things, even to the confusion and ruin of the angry, and so far involuntary, confessor. How little did that crowd of spectators know what these men were fighting about!

But if the subject was the price of a human body, whose spirit was it that enlivened it—man or woman, young or old, good or evil? The creature passed away in the middle of a large city renowned for civilisation, and even with the tread of passers-by reaching the scene, more secretly than one who perishes at sea; for, in that case, though there is none to see, there are always some to draw a conclusion. Yet, withal, we cannot say that Providence does not vindicate the importance of its creatures. That victim would, for certain, be mourned somewhere. There are even notes of woe in the grove, when the missing mate is snared by the fowler, though no one may be there to hear. It was remarked at the time when the great secret burst, and the news flew on the back of broadsheets throughout the land, that there were scarcely any direct declarations of claims. Even when conviction was heavy on the heart that a missing relative could in a certain way be accounted for, the issues were spasmed, and people only looked their thoughts. If the whisper passed, it was only among close relatives, and they kept the secret to themselves, even to the exclusion of friends. It was from this cause that the papers could not, with all their efforts, pander to the curiosity of the public by giving names. Nay, so awe-struck was that public itself, that, after the first excitement and wonder, and after Burke had paid the penalty, there seemed a wish to hurry away from both the subject and its details. They wanted back to their natural feelings and sympathies; and the hurriedness with which the crimes were laid past, with the resolution that they should not be mentioned, seemed to hold some ratio to their gigantic proportions. But the reasons which actuated the people of the time are not these by which posterity is to be influenced; for vice, whatever may be its degree, must ever be the foil of goodness, and the punishment of the wicked the sanction of virtue. It was even said by one of the newspapers of the day, that these records would at some future time form the materials out of which some Sir Walter would weave a romance. The prophecy is not justified in us. The romance-writer will come; at present, we are content with the office of chronicler.

How much we could wish that these things had never been left to us to chronicle, and how much too that what we have already said were the worst we have to say! But thus begun, it behoved that the obstinacy of these men should harden more and more; that the recklessness increased by success should, according to rule, get more and more regardless of danger, till the delirium of wickedness should throw them into the hands of justice. Already "The voice of thy brother's blood crieth unto me from the ground."

THE STUDY
FOR THE ARTIST

If these conspirators against society had limited their operations to the waifs,—a wide enough field surely in a city like Edinburgh, renowned at the time for the extent of the wide tattered fringe of the social web,—they might have remained undetected for a lengthened period;—ay, even until they had cut off hundreds; and why they left this secure area can only be accounted for by that universal law whereby the doers of evil acquire a confidence which blinds them to all sense of danger. The bold and reckless case of the young cousin was the first indication of the coming change, and we will see with what rapidity the progress was pursued in terms of that inevitable decree of Providence.

It has been mentioned that Burke had a brother of the name of Constantine, who, having driven a desultory trade something of the nature of that followed by his brother and his associate, had become a street-sweeper or scavenger, and lived in Gibb's Close in the Canongate. It never was satisfactorily established that this man was acquainted with the conspiracy, although many suspicions, especially arising out of the case of Mary Paterson, which is now to form the burden of our chapter, appeared to hang heavy upon him. For once the scene of death was changed from the old shambles to Gibb's Close. Mary Paterson, a young girl of eighteen or nineteen years of age, of remarkably handsome form, as to which we will hear more by and by, and who turned her attractions to no other use than that of *the old abuse*, had been, along with a companion named Janet Brown, lodged in the Canongate Police-office, on Tuesday the 8th of

April 1828. They were kept till four or five o'clock next morning, when they repaired to the house of a person called Mrs Laurie, where they had formerly lodged together. They had been for some time constant friends, and had more of affection for each other than is generally found among individuals of their class. The woman, who felt for them, expressed a wish that they should remain, but, for some reason unknown, they preferred another course, and went to the house of one Swanston, who sold drink. They got there a gill of whisky, and when they were drinking the spirits, their eye fell upon Burke, who was there even at that hour, busy drinking rum and bitters with the landlord. They had never seen Burke before, and made no sign of a wish to enter into conversation with him; but he, who appeared to have been watching them, came forward, and, affecting to be much taken with them, ordered an additional supply of the rum and bitters; nor did this drinking bout finish till three gills were consumed in addition to what they had drunk before. Of this drink Burke participated largely; and, indeed, it was supposed that he often wrought himself designedly up to his required point of courage by the means of liquor when he had any special work to accomplish.

In the course of the debauch, and when he discovered that the girls were of that kind who, when begun to drink, are regardless of limits, he proposed that they should accompany him to his lodgings, which he said were close by. Mary was willing enough, but her companion, Brown, shewed signs of reluctance, not probably being much enamoured of their new friend. Whereupon he roused himself to remove her scruples, by shewing money, and stating that he was a pensioner, and could keep her, Brown, handsomely, even make her comfortable for life; and that if she had any fears of the people in the house, he would stand by her against any insolence or abuse. All this attention, as Brown subsequently stated, was, as she thought, directed to her in preference to Mary—with whom, as for personal recommendations, she could not compete—in consequence of her shy and backward nature wherein she was a contrast to her friend, who was of a disposition fearless and forward. Besides, he knew from their apparent affection for each other that the one would not accompany him without the other. At length Brown gave up her scruples, and all the more readily that he made the additional offer to provide a good breakfast for them, as an earnest of all that which he had promised to do for them. Matters being now arranged, he bought from Swanston two bottles of whisky, one of which he gave to each of the two girls to carry. He then conducted them to the house of Constantine Burke, where they found that man and his wife already up, but with the fire as yet unlighted. Whereupon Burke got into a great fury, abusing the woman for negligence in not paying more attention—a feint with a meaning of which some supposed she was not altogether ignorant.

Straightway the gloomy aspect of the miserable house, the residence of so rich a pensioner, was removed by the new-lighted fire, and the woman with all activity set to work, in which she was joined by her handy brother-in-law, to produce a hearty breakfast for her lodger and guests. Tea, bread and butter, eggs and finnan haddocks, covered the table. They were now merry: the effects of the previous drink had not yet died away, while the breakfast before them, and the promises of the new friend, all tended towards a state of happiness to which the poor girls were total strangers. Meanwhile the brother, who joined in the breakfast, left shortly to proceed to his work; and the meal having been finished, with the cups and other things left remaining on the table, the two bottles of whisky were produced. The drinking again commenced, Burke still participating to a large extent, at the same time that he pressed glass after glass profusely upon the girls. The impulsive and reckless Mary, still true to her character, shewed no scruples. One glass followed another, till by and by the drug began to shew signs of a speedy triumph; but Brown was more chary, often refusing the proffered poison; not that she had any suspicions of evil design on the part of the generous pensioner, but simply because she did not wish to get drunk—a consummation so clearly impending, with two bottles on the table, and only three participants.

Burke now saw that Mary, who had fallen back on the chair all but unconscious, was safe. The next step to be taken in his scheme, which, notwithstanding the enormous quantity of drink he had swallowed, he prosecuted deliberately, was to get Brown, still comparatively sober, out of the house; and he cunningly proposed to go along with her for a walk, to revive them after their potations. The girl at once agreed, and, leaving Mary in her narcotised condition, they sallied forth; but the purpose of a walk was changed, and, inconsistently enough, Brown soon found herself in another public-house with her generous and most persevering friend. Here two bottles of London stout were ordered, along with a pie, and the girl, whose natural caution and shyness were not proof against so much seduction, drank a large share of the porter, Burke himself shewing no reluctance to participate as well, knowing not only that he could stand a great amount of drink, but that the more he took, within the limits of consciousness, if not coolness, the better able he would be for the execution of his purpose—in this instance, as it appeared, a double one, involving both the girls at the same time, or, at least, with a short intervening interval. The porter having had its due effect upon Brown, who was yet, however, far from "the point," he then induced her to accompany him again to the house they had left. Here the remainder of the two bottles of whisky was produced, Mary all the time lying almost unconscious, and only raising her head at times, and looking with stupid earnestness on the proceedings.

Now there comes up a new incident in the play, which has never been well explained. All of a sudden Helen M'Dougal, whom we might have supposed to be in Log's lodgings, who had not appeared at breakfast, and had not hitherto been seen by the girls, starts violently out of a bed. There is a whisper by Constantine's wife in the ear of Brown, that the apparition is no other than Burke's wife; and the latter immediately commenced, with all appearance of a jealous fury, to accuse the girls of having the intention of corrupting her husband. The part was so well acted, that Brown, getting alarmed, entreated forgiveness, on the plea that neither she nor Mary had known that he was married, otherwise they would not have remained in his company. The play proceeds. Helen M'Dougal breaks down: she was, she said, not angry with them, only with her husband, who was continually deserting her, spending his money on loose women, and leading a life of dissipation. She then asked them to remain, and with such apparent sincerity that Brown was satisfied, but as for Mary she was incapable of understanding a much less complicated plot. M'Dougal next turned against Burke, upbraiding him for his infidelity, taking up the things that were upon the table, dashing them into the fire, and otherwise exhibiting the height of a woman's passion. Nor was Burke indolent or regardless of this fierce onset; he retaliated, and taking up a dram-glass hurled it against her face, hitting her above the eye, and cutting, even to profuse bleeding, her forehead. At this time, or a few minutes before, Constantine's wife rushed out of the house, with the intention, as Brown subsequently supposed, of bringing Hare, but it is more probable, on the supposition of an art-and-partship, to the extent at least of knowledge, that she found some good reason for being merely absent. Immediately after her departure, Burke succeeded, with an apparent effort, in turning Helen M'Dougal to the door, and locking it after her.

Pausing a little in the midst of our narrative, we may remark, that although it was generally supposed that this quarrel between Burke and Helen M'Dougal was got up for the purpose of confusion, yet it is not easy to see how any end could have been served by it; while the cutting of the woman's face had too much seriousness about it, even as a part of the terrible drama, to admit of the theory of an entire feint. The discrepancy may be reconciled by the introduction of another passion, jealousy, but this we cannot recognise, however true, except upon the assumption that M'Dougal had some reason in her own mind to lead her to the suspicion that Burke could be unfaithful to her with the very women he intended to slay. Nor, however aggravating this may be, where aggravation seemed impossible, it cannot be held as transcending the potentialities of a nature altogether alienated from God, especially when we keep in remembrance the true character of the passion thus imputed to Burke, as being so often utterly independent of the emotion of love, in which a moral sentiment forms a necessary element. This collision, as it were, between the desire that Burke should *kill*, and another, that he should not *possess*, would produce that irregularity, as we term it, in the plot which imparts to the acting the incongruity so difficult to the analyses of the time. But while it in some measure interferes with the unity so congenial to the romancist, and which we unreasonably look for in nature, because it is more consistent with art, it presents us with a picture of human nature never before witnessed out of the domain of extravagant fiction.

At the time that Burke returned, after the locking out, Mary was lying across the bed, not having been able, even during the heat and noise of battle, to lift her head to satisfy the natural curiosity of her sex, if the curiosity itself was not altogether sopited. Burke knew the prolonged continuance of these states, proportioned as they were to the quantity of poison he had seen swallowed. So Mary is laid up as a reserve, ready for his assault at any time within the period of hours. He therefore turned his attention to the less easy subject, her companion, expressing still greater kindness to her, and pressing her by all manner of solicitation to lie down along with him in the bed from which, shortly before, his wife had so unexpectedly sprung, and who, even yet, with continued inconsistency, persisted in knocking at the door. So strong were these solicitations, and so affected was Brown with the drink she had taken, that, according to her own statement afterwards, she would have complied with his request if it had not been that she was terrified by the noise made by M'Dougal. Either supposition is possible, that he wished to gratify a purpose upon the one, and then execute his final intention upon her companion; or that he intended to immolate first the more difficult victim, and then take his own time with the other.

Fortunately the poor girl was able to resist his entreaties, as much probably through some instinctive feeling as from prudence. Anxious to get away, she expressed a wish to depart, to which Burke at first shewed no inclination, but at length, and probably under the pressure of an apprehension that, inebriated as she was, she might call for assistance, and thus deprive him of Mary, whom, as she lay still senseless, he already calculated upon as his own, he agreed to her request. He even conducted her past Helen M'Dougal, who was still upon the stair, either under the influence of her jealousy or of the old delicacy which so often took her out of the view of the final catastrophes. In all this Brown made a narrow escape, for whether Mrs Constantine Burke had really gone for the other, and perhaps greater, arch-conspirator, Hare, or not, it is certain that that fearful man arrived at Gibb's Close not long after the departure of Brown. The moment Hare arrived, and there being now no one in the house except themselves, and the unconscious Mary still lying in bed, they fell straight upon their victim. The old story again. The process was familiar to them—the energy at ready call—the execution easy. Burke springs upon the senseless victim—Hare is at his post—the heavy body pressing with the knees upon the soft bosom—the closing up of the mouth and nose—the gurgling—the long inspirations—the watchings to listen, and listen again, and examine if all was finished—the make-sure— the finish. So quickly had the process been gone through that, on Brown's return, not more than twenty minutes afterwards, Mary Paterson was lying dead, but concealed from her observation by having been flung into a corner and covered up.

It may be of interest now to trace Brown. After getting past

Helen M'Dougal, who was on the stair, about, no doubt, to watch the process inside, she went straight to Mrs Laurie's, and told her, with a laugh, that she would not remain with her, as she had got fine lodgings elsewhere; but after informing the landlady more seriously of the circumstances, she was advised to go back, along with Mrs Laurie's servant, and endeavour to get Mary removed; not, however, that either the one or the other had any fears of her ultimate safety. The accompaniment of the servant was probably another of the apparently accidental means by which the life of this girl was preserved. Half stupified as she still was, she did not recollect the name of the close in which the house was situated, and being at a loss, but still anxious about her comrade, whom she loved, she applied to Swanston for a direction to the residence of the man whom she had seen there in the morning, and with whom she and her friend had gone. The man replied, that they ought not to have gone with him, because he was a married man, and did not keep company with women of their kind, but that she would probably find him in his brother's house, in Gibb's Close. Still, so stupified was she that, after getting into the close, she went into the wrong house, where she was told that the people there kept no company with such characters, but that she would probably feel herself in the right direction by going up-stairs. They accordingly ascended, entered, and found there Helen M'Dougal, Hare, and Hare's wife. The dead prey had collected the ravens even within so short a time. Burke was absent—no doubt in Surgeon's Square; but those present, with the corpse within a few feet of them, were as unconcerned as if one among them had been engaged in throttling a chicken for dinner.

Upon inquiry for her friend, Mrs Hare rushed forward and attempted to strike Brown,—a movement not easily accounted for, except upon the supposition of a feminine way of repelling an intruder upon their secrecy, who might be dangerous; but this burst gave way to a quieter demeanour, the result of greater prudence, for the recklessness of passion is not exclusive of minor means of self-preservation. They told her that Mary had gone out with Burke, and invited her to sit down and take a glass with them, upon which the servant left. Brown now saw Hare's eye fixed upon her, and no doubt her partial inebriation was a temptation which was touching; and Helen M'Dougal continued her part of the play, by railing against her husband for going away with the girl whose dead body was actually in the room. Brown, surrounded by the three fiends, was again in danger; but, fortunately, Mrs Laurie, who had got alarmed at the report of the servant, upon what precise grounds is not known, sent back the girl to bring away Brown. No attempt was made to retain her in the presence of the servant, but she was invited to return,—a circumstance so adverse to the policy of keeping away so interested an inquirer as to be almost proof of their intention to send her after her friend, the double object of the price of her body and the seal of secrecy being the motive.

Meanwhile, changes had been going on in the house; and when Brown, in the afternoon, again called, Hare was gone—having given up his hope of the further prey, as he would calculate upon Brown's gradual return to sobriety. She was now told that Burke and Mary had never returned. Further inquiries were made, not only by Brown, but by a Mrs Worthington, with whom the two girls lived, and then another story was trumped up, to the effect that Mary had gone on the tramp with a packman to Glasgow. This story pleased Brown less than the other, which carried the inconsistency of a recovery from drunken unconsciousness in so short a time; while the tramp to Glasgow, and no intimation from that quarter, were equally unlike the habits of the girl, who could write an intelligent letter, and would certainly have done so if for no other object than to inform Brown of her departure and to claim her clothes, which still lay in Mrs Worthington's. No further intelligence was ever obtained till the great break up. The fate of Mary Paterson was meanwhile a mystery. But when we take into account the vagrant habits of these restless and changeful beings, we need make no reproach on the want of affection of friends or relatives.

We may state here that Brown believed firmly that Constantine Burke and his wife were cognisant of this affair, both from their manner at the time and the conduct of the man afterwards when she questioned him about Mary. Often, when he was at his work in the morning, she inquired if he had heard any further intelligence of her companion, but the answers were surly and snatchy,—"How the h—ll can I tell about you sort of people, here to-day and away to-morrow?" or, again, "I am often out upon my lawful business, and how can I answer for all that takes place in my house in my absence?" And so the inquiries for Mary Paterson died away for lack of satisfaction, and the only hope that remained was that some day she would cast up when weary of her wanderings with the packman.

The account which Brown gave of this unfortunate creature is touching. She admitted that she was irregular in her habits, but far from being low in her grade; and expressed her indignation at a paltry print which appeared of her, representing her in the garb of a servant, a dress in which she never appeared. She had been well educated for one in her sphere, and possessed, as we have already said, a fine person, for which she was remarkable. She was a native of Edinburgh; and her mother being dead, she was left to herself, driven along in her career by a frowardness of purpose and impulsiveness of feeling, not yet inconsistent with a warm heart and kindly affections.

The supplement of the story is given by one of the confessions of Burke. He cut the hair off her head when she was still warm. It will be remembered that he formerly dealt in this commodity, and Mary's was too long and beautiful to be given to the doctors. It might one day figure as her own on a lady of rank;—and how little she would know of the fate of her whom it had adorned, as adorning it! But to what end? Even that of the poisonous flower of Paphos, which is said to have the most beautiful petals, and to throw them the soonest away. Within four hours Burke and Hare took the body to Surgeon's Square. It was then cold enough, but had not yet got time to assume the stiffness of the dead. When uncovered, a tall lad who was along with Mr Ferguson, one of Dr Knox's assistants, expressed surprise and said that he knew the girl, and had been with her a day or two before. Sharp questions followed as to where and how she had been got, when Burke satisfied the inquirers—wondrous facility!—that he had purchased the body from an old woman at the back of the Canongate. Nor did the story finish here; So struck was Knox with the beauty and fine proportions of the body of Mary, that he invited an artist to come to the rooms to see it, for the benefit of his profession; and with the conservative instinct of an old museum collector, the curious Professor kept his favourite specimen three months in whisky. No wonder that this case roused the suspicions of the public against the doctors,—a subject we will take up in a subsequent chapter. Opinions ran high, and both sides had their reasons and their arguments, upon all which we shall attempt a judgment.

DAFT JAMIE

The work goes on, with a change of shambles. Some time after the scene in Constantine Burke's house in Gibb's Close, Burke and Helen M'Dougal removed from Log's house to that of a relation of theirs of the name of Broggan. It was never properly ascertained whether this separation was the consequence of a quarrel between the parties, or whether it was imagined that another establishment would furnish additional opportunities for carrying on the trade. The latter opinion seems to have been justified by their joint operations having undergone no interruption. Broggan's house was admirably adapted for working the conspiracy, provided the inmates could be relied on, a condition indispensable where the house consisted of only one apartment, though with a convenient dark passage into which the females could retreat as a safeguard to their feelings. If we are surprised that four individuals could be found in the world to harmonise in a confederacy for so extraordinary a purpose, we come to be appalled with wonder and dismay at the apparent facility they found in conciliating the scruples of those who could have derived but little reward for their silence. We have seen Constantine Burke and his wife acting the aiding confidants, and now we see another man and his wife brought over with apparently little difficulty. We seek for the explanation of course in the power of money, but this does not allay the wonder, if it does not rather increase it, as extending the charm of that agent even beyond what we could ever have dreamed of its influence.

The first tragedy in the new theatre involved the fate of a decent woman, the widow of a porter named Ostler, who lived in the Grassmarket, and who had died shortly before. She gained her livelihood in an industrious, if not laborious way, mainly by washing and dressing, eking it out by any desultory work she could find, sometimes in the country during harvest. She had been accustomed to visit Broggan's house in her vocation of washerwoman, and was well known to the neighbours, both from her long residence among them, and her frequent visits to the mangle at that time kept by a woman of the name of Mrs Law. One day this woman was seen to enter Broggan's house at a time when Burke was known to be there, and some of the neighbours noticed, though without paying any particular attention to the circumstance, that some time after she entered, there came from the apartment sounds of jollity, as if the inmates had got merry under the influence of drink. Burke himself exerted his musical powers, and Mrs Ostler, not to be behind, favoured the happy party with her favourite song—"Home, sweet home," which she sung in a wavering treble, not without sweetness. The symposium was no further noticed, nor was it exactly known who formed the party, but that Broggan's wife was in the house at the time, may be inferred from the fact, afterwards ascertained, that about that period she lay in of a child. From that hour Mrs Ostler was never seen. She was despatched some time after the singing of "Home, sweet home," and carried to Surgeon's Square the same evening. The ancients were fond of the subject of the shortness, the brittleness, and the vanity of human life. Homer has his soap-bubble, Plutarch his point of time, Plato his peregrination, and so forth, and the moderns imitate them. Yet, at the worst, man has generally made some little sign even at the death of a beggar. It was reserved for Portsburgh to be the place where life disappeared like a snuffed-out candle in mid-day—the hand unseen, the light scarcely missed—even the material which supplied it gone as if by magic. If Mrs Ostler was soon missed, the speculation died away under the ordinary supposition, that she had fallen into some water; and there was an end.

The first murder after the change of residence was a mere

prelude to an act—*heu! heu! vita vehementer effera et barbara!*—
altogether Cyclopic. There lived in Edinburgh in that year—
1828—an imbecile of the name of James Wilson, or, as he was
called, "Daft Jamie." His residence was in Stevenson's Close,
Canongate; but, with the exception of the night-time, he was
seldom at home, being, like most of his class, a great wanderer;
nor were his wanderings limited to the Old Town—he was seen
everywhere, and seemed never to be weary. Though evidently
deficient in intellect, he was strong and healthy in the body,
going in all weathers bareheaded and barefooted, without injury
to his constitution, and without a murmur of discontent. Never
was there a more happy creature of the kind than Daft Jamie; for
while, as we too well know, those thus afflicted were at that time,
when they were less than now under the public care, often the
objects of hatred, more often of sport and play to the young of
the lower classes, Jamie was a universal favourite. It was not that
the inhabitants of Edinburgh merely pitied him—they really
liked him. Perfectly harmless and inoffensive, and not uncomely
in his appearance, he possessed great kindliness of heart; and to
all who had occasion to be on the streets of Edinburgh, whether
early or late, he was familiar, always dressed much in the
same way,—the good-humoured, winning smile never absent
from his full round face,—always ready to salute by a peculiar
manner of taking the front lock of his hair between his finger
and thumb, nodding quickly, bowing and smiling. We can say,
from experience, that there was no resisting Jamie's smile and
the twitch of the lock, and you felt this if you had a penny in
your pocket, which was all the more readily given that he never
seemed to wish for it. Nay, he sometimes rejected money, saying
that he didn't need it, for that he had "the feck o' half-a-croon
on him." This *bonhommie* was perfectly genuine, not more
the result of the universal favour with which he was regarded
than of heartfelt kindliness, and a robust health independent of
all weathers.

Another peculiarity consisted in the importance he attached

to his brass snuff-box and spoon, which he always carried about with him, and used with great economy, and with so much of selection, that while many might be favoured with the smile and the bow, it was only a very select few, principally favourites among the young collegians, to whom he condescended to offer a spoonful of his rapee. Though undoubtedly imbecile, and incapable of any continuous mental effort, he possessed a small portion of intellect, never exhibiting any of the vagaries of his class. He kept up a correct knowledge of the days of the month and week,—a species of learning of which he was very proud,— and even went far beyond this in a certain facility he had in calculating the day on which any feast or commemoration would take place; so that to the students and boys he served as a kind of walking calendar. He had musical talents too, so well appreciated, that he was often called upon to entertain his juvenile acquaintances with a song, which he executed in tolerable style. In addition to all these recommendations, he was scrupulously clean in his person, changing his linen, it was said, three times a week; and his hands and feet, though always uncovered, appearing as having been carefully washed before he came out.

It was stated at the time that almost all the naturals then recollected on the streets of the city had met with violent or untimely deaths. There was Bobby Auld, who may yet be remembered as being a great crony of Jamie's. Bobby was killed by the kick of an ass, and fell into the hands of Dr Monro. Some others were mentioned. Nothing was more curious than to witness a forgathering between these two. They talked about affairs in general with the greatest complacency, not hesitating to criticise each other's knowledge or perspicacity— even venturing the word *fool* when the detected ignorance or error warranted the liberty. It is narrated that on one occasion Bobby and Jamie met accidentally in the neighbourhood of the Grassmarket. "It's a cauld day, Bobby." "Ay is't, Jamie. Wudna we be the better o' a dram? hae ye ony siller, man? I hae tippence."

"And I hae fourpence," says Jamie. "Ou, man," rejoins the other, "that'll get a haill mutchkin." And away they went to a neighbouring public-house, where the money having been first shewn as a necessary security, the whisky was demanded with great dignity, and placed before them But before either of them had tasted the liquor, "Lord, man," said Bobby, "did ye see the twa dougs fechtin' on the street? They're no dune yet; I hear their growling and their biting." "No," replied Jamie, "I saw nae dougs fechtin'." "It's a grand sight, though," continued the other natural. "It has lasted half-an-hour, an's weel worth seeing. I wud advise ye to gang to the door and see it, for ye'll maybe never see the like again, in this world at least." Then Jamie proceeded unsuspiciously, for he had no guile or cunning about him, to see this wonderful dog-fight; but speedily returned with the information that he could see nothing of the kind. "They'll just be dune, then," coolly observed Bobby. "But what's come o' the whisky?" said Jamie, as he opened wide his eyes on the stoup standing empty. "Ou, man," was the treacherous reply, "ye see I couldna wait." Upon Jamie's being questioned how he had revenged this foul play, his answer was in perfect character,— "Ou, what could ye say to puir Bobby? He's daft, ye ken."

Though much inferior to his crony in trickery—of which, indeed, he had none—Jamie was much his superior in intellect and knowledge. His father is said to have been a decent religious man, who took him regularly to a place of worship in the Old Town on the Sabbaths; and Jamie, perhaps from habit, continued as regularly to keep up the practice. On one occasion, when examined by a worthy elder of the congregation, it was said that Jamie not only shewed far more knowledge than could have been expected from him, but turned the tables upon his querist, putting considerably more than the old theological questions of the *enfants terribles*, which no one has been able to answer any more than our learned elder. And then, to crown all, there was the parting valediction, "If ye wud like ony mair information, Mr ——, ye ken brawly whaur to fin' me."

One morning in the month of September or early in October of the same year, Jamie was, as usual, wandering about in the Grassmarket, giving his bow and twitch of the lock to any superior person he met; for he well knew the differences of caste, considering himself far above the lowest, if not even up to the line which he drew between the giving and the withholding of the brass box and the spoon. Kindly affected towards his mother,—to whose love in return he was indebted for the clean way in which he was kept, and many attentions, for which, by a wise providence, the natural comes in, as if for compensation, to the exclusion of his brothers and sisters,—Jamie was looking for his parent. At this time he was observed by Mrs Hare,[9] who, going up as she had often done before, asked him who he was looking for. "My mither," was the answer; "hae ye seen her ony gait?" "Ay," said the woman, "she's in my house." And with this temptation she induced him to go with her. They were soon in the old den—Log's lodgings—where Hare himself was crouching for prey. Behold Jamie introduced to the court with the old honour—the fatal wink! There left with one who would take special care that he would not escape, the woman, as a provider of another kind—for she catered for life as well as death—went to Mr Rymer's shop to get some butter, and it chanced that Burke was at the time standing beside the counter. She then asked her friend, who, as we have said, was now in other lodgings, for a dram, which was accordingly handed to her by Mr Rymer, and when she was drinking it off, she stamped with her foot upon Burke's, as if to tell him that he was wanted. He knew instantly the meaning of the sign, having previously seen her leading Jamie, to use his own words, as a dumb lamb to the slaughter. The moment she departed, he followed; and when he entered, he was accosted by Mrs Hare with the words, "You have come too late; the whisky is all done." At this time, Jamie was sitting in the front room, with the cup (used for a glass) in his hand, smiling and talking, and every now and then looking round for the entry of his mother. Hare was alongside of him, and Burke took a seat opposite. It was proposed to send for another half-mutchkin, and this having been procured, they invited Jamie to the fatal back room with the window looking out on the dead wall.

On getting him into the apartment, they advised him to sit down on the front of the bed, to which he assented; and Hare's wife, after getting some of the spirits, went out, and locked the door quietly, and put the key in through an opening below it, supposed to have been made for the purpose. Now was the time to tempt Jamie with the whisky; but to their utter disappointment, they found that he would drink no more than he had done, and that scarcely amounted to a glass. It was his mother he wanted, and for her he repeatedly called, in those accents of yearning which, though coming from a youth, had, in perfect consistency with his nature, all the pathos of infantine simplicity. Alas! there was no mother there. Even the woman, who might have understood the yearning,—for she was herself a mother,—had locked him in with demons. The two men were driven out of their reckoning by Jamie's refusal to drink, and were necessitated to manœuvre; but in any view, they had a young and strong individual to deal with, and they knew, from prior experience, that unless aided by the effects of drink, they must lay their account with a desperate resistance. No effort was left untried to get Jamie to take more whisky, but still with the unsuccessful result. As yet kindly to him, he did not suspect them; and, at length, so far overcome even by the small quantity of spirits he had drunk, he lay down on the bed and fell asleep. But this state, which even in the most wicked has the appearance of innocence, was to be no guard against those to whom the old proverb so well applied,—"*Somnus absit ab oculis.*" Yes, they required to be awake, for they had *work* to do. They must kill a young, full-blooded youth, without the use of a lethal weapon, and without leaving a mark. They must wrestle to do this against the piteous appeals of innocence from one God-stricken, and who had never injured human being. They must do it with the ferocity of the striped lord of the jungle; they must do it without the help or the excuse of revenge; they must do it with the ingenuity of an artist.

Burke, who was up to the pitch of mammon's inspiration, and all the more that he had been fretted by being so far foiled by an idiot, sat watching his opportunity. The two were silent, only occasionally looking at each other, and then at Jamie, as he lay still sleeping on the bed. At length Burke said, "Shall we do it now?" to which Hare replied, "He is too strong for you yet." Burke accordingly waited a little, as probably misgivings crossed him that the conflict would be too furious to risk, and the noise might attract attention at that hour. Jamie got some more moments to live.

But this could not continue long; nor did it. Burke, become hot with impatience, suddenly threw himself upon the still sleeping simpleton, and, clutching him by the neck, attempted to strangle him. The onset roused the instinctive energies of the lad, who had sense enough to see his danger. The fear which in other circumstances would have made him run to avoid his enemies, seemed to pass into courage, and nerve him to sudden desperation. He clutched his assaulter with great force—his eye darted forth his fury—the mantling foam stood upon his lips like a lather—and throwing off the tiger with a bound, he sprang to the floor, stood erect, and awaited another onset. Nor did he wait long. Burke, in his turn, roused by opposition to the height of his wrath, again seized him, with the intention to throw him; but Jamie had the greater strength, and, besides, he fought for his life, so that he was again likely to become the master, when Burke cried out to Hare, who had hitherto kept back, as if afraid to enter into the struggle, to come forward and assist him, otherwise "I will stick a knife in you." The threat had its effect, for Hare, rushing forward at the very moment when Jamie was mastering his enemy, tripped up his heels, and laid him on his back on the floor. Not a moment was now to be lost, as the continued thumping and knocking against the furniture and the screams of the lad might reach the Close, and they must do their work, as we have said, without a knife, (which would have quickly brought matters to a termination,) otherwise no price at Surgeon's Square. The next moment saw Burke extended upon the body of the still struggling simpleton, while Hare, at his head, was engaged in the old process of holding the nose and mouth. Even after this, it was still a struggle of considerable duration. The men were sweating and breathing loud with their mere efforts to kill, and Burke, roused to fury, was often thrown off, only to spring again with greater ferocity. By and by, Jamie's struggles got weaker and weaker—relapses into stillness— wild upraisings again—spasmodic jerks of effort—those indescribable sounds which the doctors say attend cynanche— all receding gradually to the last sign. Nor did they quit their grasp till they were pretty sure they had effected their purpose. They hung over him—listened for breathings—made surety surer. Daft Jamie is dead!

This was beyond all question the most imprudent of all the acts of these terrible beings. Without supposing them mad, it is hardly possible to imagine that they could place before young men of the College, who were in the daily habit of conversing with their victim, a body which could scarcely fail to be recognised upon the instant. Yet on that very day it was put into a chest and conveyed to the rooms, where, *after examination*, it brought the price of £10. Burke, when he rose up after being satisfied that Jamie was dead, rifled his pockets, and took out the small box and the spoon, giving the spoon to Hare, and keeping the box to himself. The clothes he gave to his brothers children, who, when the bundle was unbound, fell to fighting about them; connected with which part of an atrocity which the paper will scarcely bear the impression of, is the curious fact that a baker some time after recognised upon one of Constantine Burke's sons a pair of trousers he had not long before given to Jamie. But here, again, though the mother of the lad, distracted by his sudden disappearance, ran about searching and inquiring everywhere for her poor boy, and though it was circulated that one of Dr Knox's students had affirmed that he saw Jamie on the dissecting-table, no suspicion of the manner in which he had been disposed of was ever hinted, till the final discovery, which arose out of another case. Yet it is certain that even before this event there had begun to move an under-current of uneasiness in the public mind, and even some dark hints appeared in the public prints; not that any of these pointed to anything of a defined character, but that they gradually gave rise to a suspicion that there was some great secret to be unfolded—what, no one could tell, no one even surmise—which would startle the public ear, and lay open some terrible conspiracy. Theories flew about in various guises, all as dark as they were ridiculous. Some said that there existed somewhere in the city a secret association of men, bound together by a fearful oath to avenge fancied wrongs by a crusade against society, and that the members prowled about at night for their victims, which they immolated amidst oaths and curses. Others, still more wild, whispered that the missing individuals were slaughtered and eaten by a gang of famished wretches, who having once tasted human flesh, got keen upon the zest. Sawney Bean and Christie of the Cleik rose up again, and became what they had been in olden times, the bugbears of grown children. And, however ridiculous all these fancies might appear after the disclosure of the true secret, it cannot be denied that even sensible people, who looked sharply into human nature, and were not utterly sceptical of the old legends, might, without the charge of being fanciful, be led into thoughts which they would otherwise have been ashamed of. The fact that so many individuals, old and young, had disappeared within so short a time, without a trace being left, and in many cases with their clothes lying unclaimed, remained to be accounted for, and there was no experience to guide, and no theory of human nature to explain. After all, was it possible that any supposition could transcend, yea, come up to the reality?

THE BRISK
LITTLE OLD WOMAN

It has been stated that Burke went to live in the house occupied by the man called Broggan. This house, after Broggan's departure, continued to be possessed by the lodger and his paramour. In a land to the eastward of that occupied by Hare in Tanner's Close, you reached it after descending a common stair, and turning to the right, where a dark passage conducted to several rooms, at the end, and at right angles with which passage, there was a trance leading solely to Burke's room, and which could be closed by a door, so as to make it altogether secluded from the main entry. The room was a very small place, more like a cellar than the dwelling of a human being. A crazy chair stood by the fireplace; old shoes and implements for shoemaking lay scattered on the floor; a cupboard against the wall held a few plates and bowls; and two beds, coarse wooden frames without posts or curtains, were filled with old straw and rags; so that of the money which the parties had received no part had ever been devoted to any other purpose than meat and drink, after allowing for the expense of the transitory effort on the part of the women to appear better dressed.

On the morning of a certain day of December, Burke chances again to be in the shop of Mr Rymer, where he saw a poor beggar woman asking for alms, whose brogue revealed that she was one of his country-women. The old story, you will say. Yes, alas! the old story, but with a difference. She would be garrulous—are not all poor people so?—yet the good heart admits that there is some cause for garrulity where there are wants to supply and no one willing to lend an ear. She would tell Burke, who had accosted her with the old accents of sympathy, that she had come over to Scotland to seek for her son. So straightway the sympathiser's name becomes Docherty, and he would be glad to shew kindness to his country-woman, whom he accordingly invited to his house. The proposal was accepted on the instant, and, Burke leading the way, they proceeded to this asylum, which had so miraculously come in the way of one who had no place she could call a home upon earth. On their arrival, the old play begins. Burke sets before her a breakfast, and, having left Helen M'Dougal to attend to her wants, he went straightway to find his associate, whom he informed that he had got "a shot in the house," a piece of information always welcome to that fearful man. Meanwhile Helen M'Dougal performed her part. At the very first appearance of the poor stranger she knew the fate that awaited her, and yet she set her to work in the cleaning of the house—a duty which the woman would cheerfully undertake out of pure gratitude to those who had thus generously taken in the weary wanderer and filled her empty stomach, yea, promised her harbourage for a time.

Hours passed, during which, in the absence of Burke, who would appear in due time, the two females were feminine, for they were engaged in acts which, as the natural work of their instincts, constitute so far the difference between the sexes; nor was the friendship which these acts were calculated to cement and strengthen to be weakened, in the estimation of the guest, by the arrival, in the evening, of Burke and Hare, and the latter's wife—a jolly crew, who could render compatible, again as so often before, the orgies of a wild mirth with the foreseen doom of the one round whom these orgies were celebrated. When these parties entered, there were in the house a person of the name of Gray and his wife, who had been for some time lodgers with Burke. It was necessary that these persons, who could not be trusted, should not sleep there that night, and Burke accordingly went out to seek lodgings for them, whereupon, at a certain hour, they departed, taking with them some suspicion

142

THE STORY OF BURKE AND HARE

that their banishment from their quarters did not quadrate with the excuse that a wandering beggar, albeit represented as a relative, should take their place, if they had not some other grounds, derived from particular observations, to lead them to a thought which was destined to be the original spark to raise into conflagration a long collected mass of rottenness.

On the departure of the Grays, the saturnalia preceding the sacrifice commenced, and the scene was too fraught with enjoyment for the females, always ready for scenes of excitement, to be absent. The inevitable whisky was brought, and the poor stranger, to whom it would be as warmth to a heart cold enough from poverty and privations, must partake. And now there was to be one of those apparent inconsistencies which the one string of catgut exhibits in every day of our lives. If the joyous scene was to finish by the death of her around whom, and for whom, it was celebrated, surely the more remote it was kept from observing eyes the safer; so says prudence, but prudence forgets that she belongs exclusively to the natural and the rational, and like all reasoners who argue from *egoism* to *tuism*, she expects abnormals to follow her maxims, which appear to them to be as abnorm as they are to her. So while their spirits are up, as well from the stimulant of drink as from that of the coming sacrifice, they go, whither the destined victim had preceded them, into the neighbouring apartment, occupied by a Mrs Connoway. There the scene was continued, or rather begun afresh. More drink was brought by M'Dougal, and the enjoyment was elevated into the altitudes of dithyrambism. Songs were sung, accompanied by a chorus of hoarse, broken voices, among which the *tremula* of the "brisk" little old woman mixed its quavers, till at length they all rose and danced. This scene continued for a considerable time, when they left. It was now eleven o'clock, and they were all again in their old quarters.

We have already seen that it formed a part of their plan of assault that some of the parties should quarrel and fight—the confusion thus produced being the opportunity of the assault.

And the scheme was not departed from on this occasion. In the heat of the pretended *mêlée* the little old woman, who had interfered on behalf of Burke, because he had been "kind to her," was cast down by force, for she had not drunk so much as they wanted her to do, and by keeping her senses had driven them to the necessity of the fighting prelude. This was the sign. The women, in the knowledge of the approaching struggle, hurry out of the room. At the very moment, Burke throws himself, with all the desperation of his purpose, on the body of the prostrate woman, clutching her by the throat, while his companion, bounding to his help, joins his energies in the old way, so that by the combination of powers utterly beyond resistance, she was held for full fifteen minutes, until, amidst the silence of deep hush and listening, they thought her dead. Not yet. They were deceived: there was more life than they counted upon in the little old woman, and the signs of reaction, as nature vindicated her guardship of the spirit, challenged a further effort. The weight and compression were renewed, and continued till there could be no doubt. The little old woman was dead, and in an instant after doubled up and thrown among a parcel of straw there for the purpose, in a corner of the room, between the foot of the bed and the wall.

When they were satisfied that the act had been accomplished, the women returned from the dark passage; whereupon Burke— it was now about twelve—went to the residence of Dr Knox's curator of the rooms, who lived near by, and bringing him along with him, pointed to the straw, and said, "There is a subject for you, which will be ready in the morning." After the departure of the curator, the party sat down to begin again their debauch, in the course of which they were joined by a young man called Broggan, when the revelry being continued, was carried on till four or five in the morning, at which time the two women lay down in bed, with Broggan alongside of them. Next morning, and after Hare and his wife had left for their own house, Mr Gray and his wife, who had slept there during the night, returned to Burke's, in consequence of an invitation given them by him to come to breakfast. On entering the house, they looked for the little old woman, and were surprised that she was not to be seen. Thereafter Mrs Gray having, during a search for her child's stockings, approached the bundle of straw, was met by Burke coming forward and intercepting her, by crying, "Keep out there!" with a *nod*. Broggan was then requested by Burke to sit on a chair so situated as to guard the straw, and prevent an approach; but during the day he deserted his post, and Mrs Gray, still more satisfied that there was something to be discovered, took the earliest opportunity of a search. The dissipation had driven all the actors right and left, so that at length the coast was clear. Assisted by her husband, she began to remove the straw, and the first thing she touched was the arm of the dead woman. They then examined the body, which was entirely naked, and discovered that the mouth and a part of the face were covered with blood. They had seen enough, and thought it high time to get out of that house—a purpose they were in the course of executing when they met Helen M'Dougal on the stair. Gray immediately told her he had seen the dead body, whereupon she got alarmed, implored him to hold his tongue, and said that if he did it would be worth ten pounds a week to him; but the man was honest, and replied, "God forbid that I should have that on my conscience!"[10]

Now, at last, the great secret had got into a mind true to God and nature; and here you have to mark, with gratitude to Him who takes His own time to bring evil to light and crime to retribution, the beginning of the end of all these terrible evils.

THE DISCOVERY

The records of human actions, though so often blotted by stains of blood shed by the power of money, have, as we have observed, seldom shewn more than some one individual act of violence. We exclude, of course, those which set forth the actions of regularly-organised banditti; and even there the robberies with mere violence form the general theme,—the cases of killing being the exception. Here again we see the agent not only working its wonders in the four actors, but extending its influence all around in closing up the issues of discovery. The bribe offered by Helen M'Dougal to Gray, gives us a further insight into this collateral part of the conspiracy; and while we have the young man Broggan clearly enough brought in as an additional confidant, we cannot avoid the conclusion that he too had been got over by the all-powerful agent. Nor can we account for the conduct of one more, who came into the scene at a still later period, by anything short of this paid "winking toleration."

In the evening, after Gray and his wife left the house, the body of the little old woman, which had been seen by them, was despatched to Surgeon's Square in a manner somewhat different from that of the others. Indeed, during the whole of this day, all the actors appear to have been deranged, hurrying hither and thither without definite aim, as if under the influence of a demon. The invitation to breakfast given to the Grays; the nod of Burke when he scared Mrs Gray from the straw; the imprudent watch committed to Broggan, and, above all, the leaving of the house with the body lying in the corner, and the Grays there, so evidently upon the alert, can only be accounted for on the supposition of frenzy. The new element of the discovery made by the Grays, with the threatened communication to the authorities made by the husband, was calculated to aggravate that restlessness, so much better expressed by the German word *verwirrung*. The nest was fluttered: all went to and fro, but whether it was that the main chance could not, even by all this confusion and fear, be driven from their minds, or that they saw the pressing necessity of getting the body quickly out of the house, Burke hastened and engaged a porter of the name of M'Culloch to convey the tea-chest, already procured, with its burden, to Surgeon's Square. When the man came in the evening, the body was not even put into the chest, and so confused and irresolute were the two principals, that M'Culloch was obliged to help the packing. He saw and handled the body,—forced it down with much pressure, and, even when he was on the point of getting it upon his shoulders, he noticed an oversight to which the others were blind. A part of the hair stuck out, and so, with great caution, this careful cadie took the trouble to put all to rights.

Meanwhile, the other harpies, under the prevailing restlessness and flutter, were on the watch. M'Culloch, with the burden, sallied forth by the Cowgate to find his way to the top of the High School Wynd, where he was to be met by Burke. When half way up that passage, he was joined by Burke and Helen M'Dougal, and before he got to the Square, Hare and his wife were there, so that all the four were thus, and on this occasion of delivery only, drawn together by the double motive of clutching the money, and the apprehensions enveloped in the long-reaching shadow of frowning justice. Nor did they stop there. When the burden had been deposited, and M'Culloch requested to go to Newington, where Dr Knox resided, to get his five shilling fee for his winking toleration, they all set off together, and, though there was some straggling and separating, the women never lost sight of the men. Arrived at Newington, Dr Knox's curator took the principals, along with M'Culloch, into a public-house, the women hanging about outside on the watch, and a part of the price, to the extent of £7, 10s. having been paid and divided, the whole party returned to the city.

While all this was going on, the man Gray, having been finally moved to his purpose of informing the authorities of what he had witnessed, and having also seen the removal, had repaired to the Police-office, where, after waiting some time, he saw the officer, John Fisher. To him he detailed what he and his wife had witnessed.[11] The bringing in of the "brisk" little old woman—her good health—the manœuvre to get him and his wife to sleep at Hare's—so much of the orgie with its dancing and singing as he knew—the disappearance of the stranger in the morning—the discovery of the body under the straw—the blood upon the mouth—the bribe of £10 a-week—the removal of the body. Whereupon Fisher, after despatching his informant before him, repaired to the premises, but he went with no other thought in his mind than that Gray was influenced by spite;— so near again was the conspiracy to an escape from detection. Nor did even what Fisher found and heard tend to awaken him. On getting to the house, he met Burke and M'Dougal, with Gray and another man called Finlay, coming up the stair, and having told Burke that he wanted to speak to them, they all returned to the room. Fisher then began his interrogations.

"Where are all your lodgers?" he said, directing himself to Burke.

"There is one," replied he, pointing to Gray. "I turned him and his wife out for bad conduct."

"But what has become of the little woman who was here yesterday?" he continued.

"She's away."

"When did she leave?"

"About seven o'clock in the *morning*, and Hare will swear he saw her go."

"Any more to swear that?"

"Oh, a number!" replied Burke, insolently.

Whereupon Fisher began to look about the house, and especially the bed, where he saw many marks of blood.

"How came these there?" he inquired at Helen M'Dougal.

"Oh," replied she, confidently, "a woman lay-in there about a fortnight ago, and the bed has not been washed since; and as for the little old woman, she can be found. She lives in the Pleasance, and I saw her to-night in the Vennel."

"And when did she leave this?" he rejoined.

"About seven o'clock *at night*," replied the incautious Helen.

Upon this small discrepancy depended the further prosecution of the inquiry, and, consequently, either the present discovery of the conspiracy, or the continuation of it, with, probably, if possible, increased atrocity, for Fisher was satisfied as to the blood as well as to Gray's spite, and, according to his own assertion, came to the resolution of taking Burke and M'Dougal to the Office, *only* on the mere chance ground of their difference about a time of the day. On arriving before the Superintendent, Fisher mentioned what he had seen, and also what he thought; but the superior, quickened by the mention of the blood, which so far, hypothetically, at least, harmonised with Gray's story, took another view. Yet how far was he from suspecting that he had in his very hands the key to that chamber of horrors, the untraceable existence of which had for a time produced so much deep-breathing oppression in the public mind! He immediately paid a visit to the house, along with the police surgeon, Mr Black, and Fisher himself. There they found a stripped bed-gown, which Mrs Law, who came in, stated belonged to the little old woman, and in addition to what Fisher had seen, a quantity of fresh blood, mixed with *fifteen or sixteen ounces of saliva*, among the straw now under the bed, but which, as we have seen, lay formerly between the end of the bed and the wall.

On the following morning, the same three parties proceeded to Dr Knox's rooms in Surgeon's Square, and having got the curator formerly mentioned, who felt no hesitation in assisting their inquiries, they were led by him to the cellar. "There is the box," said he, "but I do not know what is in it." On opening it they found the body of a woman quite naked, and Gray having then been sent for, came and identified it as that of the little old woman. Thereupon the body and box were conveyed to the Police-office; and on the day following an examination was conducted by Dr Christison and Dr Newbigging, assisted by Mr Black, which, according to the conjectures of the first, who as yet knew nothing of the real manner of death, harmonised wonderfully with the *res gesta*. There were several contusions on the legs, probably caused by the heavy shoes of the assailants—another on the left loin—another on the shoulder-blade—one on the inside of the lip, the consequence of pressure against the teeth, and two upon the head, probably from being knocked against the floor in restraint of efforts to rise. Above all, as an index to the *modus*, there was a ruffling of the scarf skin under the chin, and as a proof of the *force*, a laceration of the ligaments connecting the posterior parts of two of the vertebræ, whereby blood had effused among the spinal muscles as far down as the middle of the back. There was also blood oozing from the mouth and nose. The body appeared to be that of a healthy person, all the organs of the vital parts being unusually sound. From all which, Dr Christison, and also the two other doctors, drew the conclusion, that the woman had met with a violent death by means of throttling—a form indicated by the ruffling of the skin below the chin as more likely than that of smothering or suffocation. Nor was this conclusion liable to be affected by the fact stated by Mr Black, that many of the intemperate people of the city, and so many that he had seen six cases in the Police-office at one time, were often on the eve of death, nay, altogether deprived of life, through accidental suffocation from drink, produced by chance obstruction of the mouth, or lying with the face on a pillow.

All this information having been obtained, the authorities were at length roused, and the Lord Advocate, it is said, saw at once that he was on the eve of a great discovery, which would explain the recent disappearances. All secrecy was imposed upon officials, yet in spite of the precaution, parts of the story got currency among the people, and, offering a solution as they did of the prevailing mystery, deepened the awe, while they stimulated the curiosity not of the city only, but the kingdom. Hare and his wife were laid hold of, and inquiries in every direction set on foot and prosecuted. Recourse was had to the culprits, in the hope that some one or more of them would confess, but at first there was no success in this direction, each of them maintaining that they knew nothing of the death of the woman, or the fate of any of the prior victims. On the 3d and 10th of November, Burke and Helen M'Dougal, finding that one fact could not be denied, that a dead body was found in their house, issued declarations whereby a story was trumped up to the effect that it was brought there by a stranger, who called one day to get some work performed by the former; but these were disregarded as inconsistent and ridiculous, and the authorities were left to their scent. The evidence of the Grays was of great importance, and other people were found who could speak to isolated facts. Hugh Alston could swear that at half-past eleven on the night of the 31st of October, when he was going to his house, in the same land where Burke resided, he heard a noise coming from the latter's room—men quarrelling and fighting—(the feint preceding the onslaught)—and amidst the uproar the peculiar voice of a female crying murder, then after some minutes the uproar diminished, and he heard a cry as if proceeding from a person or animal that had been in the act of being strangled. This circumstance recurred to him, and struck him forcibly next evening, when he heard that a body had been found in that house.

Additional information was got from Mrs Connoway, who occupied a room on the right hand of the main passage leading to that other which terminated in Burke's apartment. She remembered that, on Hallowe'en night, Burke brought in with him a little old woman; that, on subsequently going into his house, she saw her there sitting by the fire supping porridge and milk, and upon her saying, "You have got a stranger,"

M'Dougal replied, "Yes, a Highland woman, a friend of Burke's." In the darkening, the woman came into her house, and she was surprised to hear her calling Burke by the name of Docherty, wherein she corrected her. By and by, Hare and the two women followed, one of the latter having a bottle of whisky, part of which the stranger partook of along with the rest. Thereafter they got merry, when they all rose and danced, the little old woman among the rest. When the others left, the woman remained till such time as Burke, who was out, should return to his own house, because she trusted to him for protection. During the night she was disturbed by a terrible noise as of a fight; and in the morning, about nine or ten, having gone ben, she found collected Mrs Law, Young, Broggan, M'Dougal, and Burke, the last drinking whisky, and sprinkling it over the bed and the straw, and M'Dougal singing a song. On inquiring where the little old woman was, she was told by Helen that she had kicked her out, because she was "ower freendly" with her husband. Towards six she was called upon by Mrs Gray, who having previously told her of the dead body, asked her to go in and see it, but when she complied, she got so frightened that she turned and ran out. Further on, her husband told Burke that it was reported that he had murdered the woman; on hearing which he laughed very loud, as well as M'Dougal, who was present, and then said, he "did not regard what all Scotland said of him." Nor did he seem to be in the smallest degree afraid. This information afforded by Mrs Connoway was corroborated to a certain extent by Mrs Law, who occupied a room in the main passage opposite to that of the former; and Broggan was willing to go so far as to admit certain things, among the rest, the charge of sitting on the chair opposite to the straw.

Withal though this evidence could leave no doubt on the mind that murder had been committed, it did not amount to proof against any particular person. All that pertained to the disposal of the body at Surgeon's Square was frankly told by the curator; but, with this exception, there was much to complain of as regards the doctors. Knox and his assistants, all of whom shewed from the beginning a marked, if not determined, refusal to help the authorities in the furtherance of justice. But if all the testimony that could be procured in support of the charge in this case was insufficient, the deficiency was still greater in regard to those of Mary Paterson and Daft Jamie, for unfortunately no one, with the exception of the accomplices and the gentlemen in Surgeon's Square, had seen their dead bodies, or could even say they were dead, so that the *corpus delicti* was literally little better than a myth. The authorities were therefore placed in a very trying position. The people cried for vengeance; and the Lord Advocate could only respond, "The decrees of the blind goddess are not gropings in the dark;" and he moreover, said, that an ineffectual trial, followed by an acquittal, would not only be injurious to the interests of justice, damaging to the prestige of official dexterity, but dangerous to the country, in the humour in which the inhabitants of Edinburgh felt themselves. That humour had often shewn itself before. The example of the Porteous mob was not only a lesson, but, as regards the crimes, a derision; and it was just as certain as the death of the brisk little old woman, that the big old Edinburgh would take the blind lady into their own hands, and if she would not *see* that it was right that these four persons should be hanged, whether on a barber's pole or not—they would extract her cataract or cure her *amaurosis* for the purpose, and then immolate the criminals at her altar.

From this anxiety with which the Lord Advocate was oppressed, there was an impending relief. The diligent officials, all straining for the satisfaction of the people, the vindication of justice, and the comfort of their superior, were continually attempting the prisoners, and at length it was discovered that the crafty, cruel, and cowardly Hare, and also his wife, were beginning to shew signs of inclination to buy their lives at the expense of those of their perhaps less guilty associates. The leer of the "fearful man," when the proposition was made to him, was a repetition of the old satisfaction when a "shot was in the house," and it is not unlikely that he chuckled at the rising thought of sending him to the college for the benefit of science and the good of his fellow-creatures; nor was the indication either unnatural to him or fallacious to the public. In a short time he declared himself, but on the condition of a firm bargain. The "shot" must be paid for by the price of immunity to his person and that of his wife.

When this information reached the law officers of the Crown, they hailed it with that amount of satisfaction which might be felt when a man procures by chemical agents from pollution the means of reproducing health. It could be doubted by no one that the evidence of such a *socius criminis* as Hare, or *socia criminis* as the amiable Mary, would be worth less than the value of an old song, insomuch that while the old song *might* be true, the words of Hare, in a transaction where he himself was concerned, could *not possibly* be true. He would represent, and the people knew it, the Janus head with one face looking simpering peace to himself, and the other bloody war to his friend. Nor was this foreknowledge of the man, founded as it was upon such an array of actions, belied by the result. The precognition was, from beginning to end, a long train of lies, wherein he represented himself as a good, easy soul—his wife as well—who allowed Burke to have his own way, neither advising him nor assisting him, only not obstructing; and even where he could not avoid some confession of participation, attributing his weakness to the easiness of his nature. How innocently he took a little liquor so as to make him, not drunk, but merely put him in a sort of "drunkish way!" How benignantly he sat on the chair at the side of the bed when the ruffian Burke was fighting like a tiger to squeeze the life out of the little old woman! As for the money, he merely accepted it—never earned it; and who refuses money? So glaring was the falsehood of the man's statement, and not less that of his wife, that the Lord Advocate was by no means sure of a verdict. *Socii criminis* have shades of character, but they are only to be believed when they shew penitence, and strike with vigour their own persons; but Hare only held on and kicked out; and a jury true to their consciences might, after all, become disgusted, and find a verdict of "Not proven."

THE COMPLICITY
OF THE DOCTORS

If the world is rife in unknown crimes, it is still more rich in winking toleration, insomuch as there is generally several winkers to one actor, and the former are of various kinds, while the latter is limited in his passion. Some are cowardly accorders, who favour the crime which they have not courage to commit; others are selfish, and expect benefit from their convenient nictation; and some there are who would be injured by the virtue of others having its own reward. So it is that the world, notwithstanding grave faces and simpering moralities, contains within its circumference only a trifle fewer rogues than inhabitants, the residue being God's own—stern beings who have fought the devil at his own weapons and conquered. These have a certain price in another place, where the golden streets are happily not liable to be coined; but here they are of small account, where money is the measure of a man's worth. We have already seen that even such men as Burke and Hare had their sympathisers and secret-keepers; but these were low, and therefore liable to be tempted; and it may be said that we have different men to judge when we go to the halls of science and seek for the winking tolerators of wholesale murder.

So far we admit, and we would be sorry indeed to do these men and youths injustice. We know that great authorities, such as *Blackwood*, and smaller ones, such as Colonel Cloud, accused them of art-and-partship as resetters, and that the public at large did not hesitate even to vociferate anathemas before a regular trial—with the devil's advocate to plead for them—qualified them for excommunication by book, bell, and candle. All this

156

goes for nothing with us at a time when it was said the fire of passion would be allayed, and sober reason exert her authority.[12]

It is fair, and even necessary, to assume as a fact, which, indeed, we have seen established by the practice of "Merry-Andrew" and the "Spune," that the disinterring craft were in the habit of purchasing dead bodies from poor lodging-keepers or relatives, in all which cases the bodies would be very different in appearance from those procured in the ordinary way. We suspect, from the nature of the Scotch character, with its sympathies and friendships, that those examples were not at any time many; and the best evidence of this is, that under such an easy system, the resurrection trade, always difficult and precarious, would not, especially after the indictment of Dr Pattison of Glasgow in 1814, have been so assiduously prosecuted. Such a system, too, depending upon the character of a people and the feelings of individuals, must be supposed to have been under the regulation of those natural, or, if you like, unnatural, laws to which all organic beings are subjected. If, during a period of a decade, examples of such purchase and sale were only one or two in a year, even increasing *paulatim et gradatim* to three or four, we would not be prepared for a sudden increase starting up all at once in one year to from sixteen to twenty; and there were many people who calculated the number in our "Court of Cacus" at thirty. We may insist here a little upon this view, because, amidst all the outcry against Knox and his assistants, it was never taken into account.

Nor could this sudden rise have appeared the less startling to any mind below that of an idiot, that this new trade was not spread over a great number of persons—and nothing less than a *very* great number could have sufficed for watching, ferreting, persuading, bribing—overcoming all the prejudices arrayed against an act of sale—but was altogether engrossed by two poor squalid Irishmen, who had come into the trade by a leap, and all but superseded the old experienced hands. If we were to make the supposition, that now, or at any other period in the history of Scotland, two Irishmen had taken it into their heads to set up a trade of this kind in the city of Edinburgh, we would soon come to an estimate of their success, if the doubt would not rather be, that if they got one body in the course of a whole year, it would be no less a wonder than a shame. Nor was there any reasons which might have led the recipients in the Square to suspect that these two solitary individuals were merely the agents or hands of a "dead-body company," or a joint-stock affair, with one of the crack names, "Association for the purpose of purchasing dead bodies, for the benefit of science and the human race," a supposition which alone could have reconciled men with eyes in their heads, and brains in those heads, to the anomaly before them.

But above all, that which had so much the appearance of justifying the public rage, was the state in which the contents of these bags, boxes, and chests were presented to the purchasers. One example may serve for the whole. There was no reason for supposing that more violence was expended upon Mrs Docherty than upon the others, if we are not rather to suppose that the younger and stronger cases required more vigour, as presenting more resistance. Even in the weakest cases, the *præsidia vitæ* upon which nature has expended so much labour are not to be overcome by external force weakly exerted, and without leaving marks easily detected, even by the unlettered in anatomy; but we have only to mention the case of Daft Jamie, who fought manfully to the end, as an example of the necessity of leaving upon the body even greater signs of violence than those presented to the eyes of Dr Christison. Taking the little old woman as a fair medium between the young and the old, the weak and the strong—you may remember the examination report: contusions and bruises everywhere, extravasation of blood, blotches of the same crying evidence, and finally the Lydian test of the abraded skin of the throat,—while less or more of these marks must have appeared in every one of the sixteen known cases, we cannot even suppose a solitary example of one where they could have been altogether wanting; and this led many to wonder at the time how the men preferred violence, with so many chances of detection, to the soffana death-drops of some subtle poison, the effects of which were far less likely to be discovered by mere anatomists, curious about structure only, and so far removed from the duty of a *post-mortem* examination. With no pathological views in their minds, they never would have dreamt of smelling for prussic acid, or searching for the ravages of green vitriol or arsenic, any more than they thought of drawing up their noses under the effluvia of whisky—an evidence which was never absent, and could not be mistaken, and must have led to the curious conclusion that all the bodies sold by friends were those of drunkards, and drunkards alone.

These contusions, and the invariable thumb-mark on the throat, were, according to the gentle supposition, to be overlooked by men all on the alert to see the cloth taken off—curious investigators into the arcana of nature—most zealous inquirers into the structure of the human body—among whom anything abnormal, or departing from ordinary laws or appearances, produced a speculation, fraught not only with the ardour of science, but the contentious conceit of young aspirants. Nay, these sharp professional eyes were not the first examiners, for they came after the decision of the mercantile, which scanned the value to fix the price. We are aware that there never was an enunciation, not excepting the famous *what is is*, without the condition of being liable to argumentation, and we are far from wishing to deprive these men of their defence; but that they should have treated as they did the imputation cast upon them, of, we do not say winking toleration, but something like pretty wide-awake suspicion, as an Argive calumny, pointed with venom and shot by passion, was going to the other extreme. Offended innocence is not always the meek thing represented by poets, yet it seldom takes on the form of a man at a window[13] threatening to shoot the officials of the law if they dared to question for the ends of justice so innocuous and ill-used a victim of public prejudice.

In all we have said we have assumed that these suspicions were to cast up their shadows in the magic-lantern of minds, quite free from any recollections or surmises of any body having ever been offered, in the Square or neighbourhood, which could be said to have come to a violent death. The assumption which was set forth at the time was not true, for it turned out to have been pretty well known—and what professional scandal is unknown to students?—that some six months only before, and when the Irishmen were in full feather, the body of a female was offered for sale by some ill-looking men—we do not say, as was said, of Burke's gang—to the assistant of another teacher of anatomy in the city. The men were not known to him as regular "Spunes," but as a subject was required, he consented to accept of it, after being satisfied that it suited him. They said that they had it now, and would bring it to the rooms in the evening, between nine and ten o'clock, and at the appointed hour they made their appearance, with a porter bearing the sack. The burden was taken in and turned out of the bag, when it proved to be the body of a woman of the town, in her clothes, with her shoes and stockings on. The startled assistant proceeded at once to an examination, when he found a fracture on the back part of the head, as by a blow from a blunt instrument. "You d——d villains," cried this honest doctor, "where and how did you get this body?" Whereto one, with much self-possession, replied, "It is the body of a w——e, who has been *popt* in a row in Halkerston's Wynd; and if you don't take it, another will." The assistant then proposed, with the intention of having them apprehended, that they should wait till he sent for his principal; but the men, taking alarm, made off with their cargo, and soon found a less scrupulous customer. This statement, which was given on authority, was accompanied by an assurance that equally suspicious cases were by no means rare.

In addition to this preparation of the mind, as it may be called, to look suspiciously on introductions coming out of the regular way, with the admission made that they had not been exhumed, and with the inevitable traces of violence which could not be blinked, there was the peculiarity on which, perhaps, the greatest stress was laid, that in one of the cases, at least, there was a recognition of the individual by one of the students as having been seen and conversed with by him, in terms of more than ordinary intimacy, only the night before, or at least a very short period, countable by hours. We allude to Mary Paterson, "the study for the artist," who, though naked, was said to have made her appearance on the table *en papillote*—not to be believed—but who, for certain, attracted so much observation, yea, admiration, that the recognition by the youth could not have fallen as an idle brag. The case of Daft Jamie, the collegians' favourite of almost every day's fun, was so much stronger, that there seemed no mode of accounting for the pure innocence of Surgeon's Square, except upon the supposition that all the students had, in the course of a day, been merged in some Lethe. No great wonder that the most zealous defenders of the craft were here contented with a simple shaking of the head, for, to be sure, even the devil's advocate has not an interminable tether.

These charges are very practical, and even to us, at this distant period, who would be regulated by reason and truth, and cannot be under the influence of passion, are hard bones. Independently of our estimate of youths—putting Knox out of the question,—of good birth and parentage, whose generous hearts would revolt from the thought of a guilty cognisance,— some of these assistants who came in contact with Burke, "and no questions asked," have risen to rank in their profession, and bear a high character for honesty and humanity. "They ken their ain ken;" but their negative defence leaves their friends to the slough of mere metaphysics. We all know that mysterious attractiveness and repulsiveness of the mind which makes such fools of even the most practical of mankind. The man would not look through Galileo's telescope, because he knew beforehand that there was nothing to be seen; but he did no more than every man does every day he lives. We all know that we may look, and not see, hear, and not understand; yea, though the image of the outer thing may be in black and white on the back of the eye, and the words play their intellectual tune on the drum of the ear, you may neither see the one nor hear the other. The bird-lime of acceptance is not present, and there is even more—an absolute recusancy in proportion to some reigning wish in the form of what we call a prejudice. All this is alphabetic, and we might go deeper and get lost, but there is no occasion. The truth is, that these medical students had a strong wish for subjects. This rose out of another wish, that for knowledge, and this again came out of one behind, a wish to shine or make money,—the benefit to mankind being only that thing which we all understand when we hear people getting philanthropical in recommending their leather, as contributing to the good of the eternal sons of God. Then the next truth is, that they *did* suspect, and becoming the paradoxes which so many unconsciously become, did not *know*, in the sense of an apprehension, that they suspected. When the thought sought entrance to the mind, always under the cogency of the repulse of unwillingness, it was either thrown out or dissolved; to all which the authority of their leader or lecturer contributed, and not less the generosity of their own hearts, naturally seeking uniformity, and averse to think so ill of human nature, as was required to be implied in an atrocity never before heard of in the world. If the thought had ever come so strong upon them as to have amounted to an active conviction, why, then they must have glided into the crime of winking toleration, and to that, we verily believe, they never came. There were only three of these young men who took an active charge. If there had been a score, we might have conceded that one, perhaps two, might have been found among them capable, by the predisposition of an evil nature, to have quietly succumbed to the force of such startling appearances; but judging of the proportions according to what we find among men, we require a large number for the successful selection of the devil's own. In short, they were very much in the position of resetters, who, standing in great need of the article, take refuge from a suspicion which would injure them in the fallacious eloquence of the naturally selfish heart, and casting up behind them intervening obstructions to the light—a kind of weakness into which all mankind are less or more liable to fall, and against which they are ready to recoil when the passion of possession decays. It requires only superficial looking to bring us to the conclusion, that the world is a great collection of "wee pawns," every man resetting some thought or feeling, false in itself, and improperly come by, and wrongfully retained. The difference here lies in the fact, that we have not yet come to hold this a crime, nor are we likely to do so till regeneration comes wrapt up in the world-wide cloak of the millennium.

In what we have said, we refer only to those who superintended the division of the bodies and the work of the rooms, and were those who came in contact with Burke. As for the curator, who is still a respectable inhabitant of Edinburgh, and upon whom the short-lived blind fury of some newspapers of the time fell, with much surprise to himself, and much indignation elsewhere, he was, of all the parties concerned, the most free from blame; nor did any one but himself come forward and assist the authorities in the prosecution. Nay, it is understood that, under a passing reflection that the number of apparently unexhumed bodies brought by these men required explanation, he mentioned the circumstance to his principal, and that gentleman silenced him at once by the statement that they had long known of the practice of sale and purchase, and so the suspicion passed away. And, indeed, in reference to them all, it requires to be kept in view that Dr Knox's great characteristic was his desire to subjugate all people to his will; and every one knows the insidious power of authority. Accordingly, in so far as regards that gentleman, left to the active fury of a mob which he braved, and to the suspicion of more thinking people whom he tried to conciliate, we have little to say. His whitewashing process, consisting of the printed judgment of his conduct by a committee of eminent men, went a considerable length in his favour, and yet did not save him from almost general suspicion. The evidence was all of his own selection; the world never knew what it consisted of; and though we are bound to admit that the umpires vindicated the privilege of searching and satisfying themselves, he behoved to be still their director, and, if he chose, their obstructor. Perhaps those who knew the man the best, and those who knew him the worst, were the least satisfied,—the latter being under passion, and the former aware of a power of conciliation and persuasion under the guidance of a self-love and power of will not often to be met with, and all this professedly not regulated by any sense of religion or respect for public morals. In him we have seen already the one gut-string playing several airs, but without a touch of pity: the soft was not indeed his forte, his preference lying in the direction of those examples we have already given—the joke upon Professor Jameson, the poisoned satire upon Liston, the egotism among the Taymouth Castle guests, the adulation of the Marquis of Breadalbane. Nor can we forget, beyond all, the admitted perspicacity of one of the best anatomists of his time, which, if it had been called in question in an ordinary autopsy, with the most recondite appearances of poison or violence, would have been vindicated by a power and success, accompanied by a bitterness not often witnessed among scientific men. In his letter of 11th January 1829, to the curator of his rooms, he said, "All such matters as these subside in a short time." "Not so," added the editor of the *Mercury*; "such matters cannot subside till such time as he (Dr Knox) clears himself to the public satisfaction." Time, we fear, has shewn the falsehood of the one statement, and the hopelessness of the other. The same suspicion remained, yea, remains still, and we fear will go down through all time with the record of a story destined ever to be the greatest example of man's wickedness, when left to his idol, that has ever appeared.

THE TRIAL

In November 1828, a citation was served upon William Burke and Helen M'Dougal to appear before the High Court of Justiciary to be held at Edinburgh, the 24th day of December, at 10 o'clock forenoon, to underlie the law in the crime of murder, on three separate indictments. The first comprehended the case of Mary Paterson, as having occurred in the preceding month of April in the house of Constantine Burke; the second—that of James Wilson, or Daft Jamie—in October of the same year in Log's house, situated in Tanner's Close; and the third—that of Madgy, Marjory, or Mary M'Gonegal or Duffie, or Campbell, or Docherty—in November, in Burke's house, Portsburgh. The libel contained also a list of a great number of articles of dress worn by the victims, and identified, and, among others, Mrs Docherty's gown, and Daft Jamie's brass snuff-box and spoon.

The presiding judge of the Court at that time was the Lord Justice-Clerk Boyle; the other judges, Lords Pitmilly, Meadowbank, and M'Kenzie; and the prosecutor, Sir William Rae, Lord Advocate. The leading counsel for Burke was the Dean of Faculty, that for M'Dougal, Henry Cockburn, James Tytler being the Crown agent. The witnesses were fifty-five in number—the two principal, Hare and his wife, received as king's evidence in the characters of *socii criminis*. The panels having taken their places at the bar in the midst of a crowded court, filled long before the opening of the doors by people who had the privilege of influence, and whose numbers were only as a trifle in comparison of the mass outside, Mr Patrick Robertson, one of Burke's junior counsel, made a technical objection to the reading of the indictment, which was overruled. A defence was then lodged for Burke, and supported by the same counsel, on the ground that it was contrary to the law of Scotland to combine in one libel so many charges and two separate panels. The argument, which was a long one, involving points of law and practice, was followed up by the Dean of Faculty, and answered by the Lord Advocate, with this result, that the judges, with the consent of the public prosecutor, agreed to limit the charge to the case of Docherty, and thus limited, the proceedings went on. The various witnesses, forming, however, a very small portion of the whole fifty-five cited, appeared in succession to give their evidence. Every word uttered by every one was caught by ears strung to the highest pitch of sensibility; and throughout the entire day, the deep silence, more like that of a death-chamber than a court, was as much the expression of curiosity as of awe—reminding one, too, of the stillness of an audience where the feelings are claimed by oppressed virtue with the encircling meshes in which innocence is to be involved by death getting closer and closer as the scenes succeed. The interest lay in the gradual development, while the heart was affected by all the different passions which, changing from pity for the victims to hatred of the murderers, were kept in continual agitation. Over all, there was the oppressive awe inspired by the presence of the fearful men and women, as if they had been demons of monstrous forms and powers placed there under restraining bonds. At several times,—and especially when Hare described the screigh of the little old woman which preceded that ten minutes' agony in which she lay under the pressure of Burke— Hare being all the while, according to his lie, sitting coolly looking on,—you might have heard deep sighs escaping from strong hearts, in spite of resolutions to restrain them. Even then the grateful creature, who seemed to have trusted Burke alone, and defended him in the preceding sham fight, was only "dead a wee," and the process was to be resumed. But even this effect was transcended, if possible, by the very manner in which the witness stated how the victim was presently stripped, and after being bound neck and heel, was cast, mangled and bloody, among the straw in the angle between the bed and the wall. The dominant idea seemed to bring into light all the surrounding objects—the table pushed aside, the old chairs, the squalid bed marked with the blood of prior victims, the women listening with expectation in the long dark passage, the two men panting after the struggle, and bringing forth on the top of their long-drawn breath ribald jokes, and even accomplishing a laugh,—all followed by the rush in of the women, and the resumption of the drink, the song, and the dance.

To the greater part of those assembled in the court, all this was comparatively new, for great secrecy had been observed by the officials. Yet the effect of the great scene did not diminish, or rather, it increased, the interest in the particulars,—the suspicions of the Grays—the restlessness of the murderers under the impression of impending discovery—the lies about having turned the poor creature out because she was too intimate with Burke—the start of Mrs Gray when she seized the arm of the body among the straw—the lifting up of the head by her husband, and the recognition of the features of the woman who had been dancing and singing so short a time before—then the pressing down into the tea-chest, and the sally forth of the whole gang to Surgeon's Square, from thence to Newington for the price. And as in a tragedy we find collateral lights thrown in by the scintillations of genius to increase the effect of the stronger scenes, so here these were not wanting. How much the sympathy for the little old woman was increased by the love and gratitude she expressed for her benefactor, Burke, when contrasted with the savage eyes that glared upon her as she lay under his death-grasp! Another of these smaller traits going to the aid of the general effect, was the fact stated by the prior witnesses, that when she met Burke, she was going about seeking for her son; and this yearning had only given place for a little to the new feeling of gratitude with which she strove to repay the sympathy of him who had from the first made up his mind to slay her. It was even whispered that that son was in the court listening to the fate of his mother; and, whether true or not, it did not fail of its contribution.

Nor was all this exclusive of that mingling of the grotesque with the serious which the playwright, following nature, resorts to for deepening his shadows. The face of Hare, as he stood in the witness-box, seemed incapable of the expression of either seriousness or fear. The leer was irrepressive, even had there been a wish within to repress it—and there was none; and as for any effect from without, that seemed equally unfelt by him, if the gloom and awe which pervaded the court did not rather increase an inborn propensity to be humorous. He could not say seriously that the woman was dead, only that she was "dead a wee,"—nor that he was drunk, only "drunkish-ways;" and when asked if the word "shot" implied murder amongst the crew, he answered, as impeaching Burke, "amongst him;" so that if you took his looks and words together, you could not, if you had read the accounts of the classic satyrs, avoid the impression that, like these creations of the poets, he was condemned to an eternal grin of self-satisfied sarcasm against the whole human race. Nor, strange as it may seem, did he appear to consider this as incompatible with a wish to produce the impression that while he could mix in and receive the price of murders, he was only (as we have already said) an indolent and easy spectator—a kind of lover of the play, but not an actor. It appeared, indeed, evident that it required only an indication on the face of his questioner to prompt him to laugh, and this was probably all that was wanting to complete an exhibition which no one could ever forget.

The appearance of his wife, who had a child in her arms, was scarcely less impressive, but not from any characteristic indicating the successful cunning displayed by the husband. She could scarcely contain herself. You saw the bloated virago always appearing from under a bunchy and soft mass, with small fiery eyes that peered about in every direction, as if she felt she had come there to favour the judges, who were bound accordingly to admire her. Like most of the famous examples of her sex renowned for cruelty, it was clear she could be as mild as gentleness itself; and it was only when she came to the great scene when she saw Burke lying on the body of his victim, and "flew out of the house" because of her delicacy, and stood in the passage "quite powerless," unable to "cry out," that you could come to form a true estimate of that combination of the devilish and the soft, which so much distinguishes the wicked of the one sex from those of the other. She admitted that she knew very well that Burke was murdering the woman, because she had seen "such tricks before;" yet she had "no power to remove herself from the passage;" and whenever the counsel or judge wished to know whether the victim screamed or shewed any indication of violent suffering, her mouth would give out nothing but soft words, so afraid was she to see anything "come upon the woman," all the while that the fiery scintillations escaped from these small eyes. To the next question, she admitted that she went for the tea-chest, trying to save herself by the qualification that Burke said it was to hold old shoes; and then, in a few minutes after, "she knew that the body was put into that box." Nor was the audience less struck with the manner in which she used the infant as an instrument to produce pity, and a mean of fence against searching questions. The poor creature was under the influence of hooping-cough, and as the long choking inspirations came every now and then ringing through the court, they reminded the audience of the strangling of the victims, and seemed to be intended by God as a mysterious kind of sign. She was not only a woman but a mother; and should not this produce sympathy even to one who had fought the fight of the drunken virago in the street of Portsburgh, been art-and-part in a dozen of murders, who had led the kind-hearted simpleton as a dumb lamb to the slaughter, and had so often watched under the hush of breathless expectation for the sign when the work was done, and then hung, like one of those fabled creatures called "Furies," round the slayers and the slain, to get her part of the prey?

When the witnesses were all examined, there ran through the court a whisper, "Where are the doctors?" and well there might, for in all that crowd you could not have got half-a-dozen who did not think these men nearly as culpable as the principal actors. It was known that their names had been placed on the back of the indictment as witnesses, but a very small amount of consideration might have satisfied any one that, whether appearing for the prosecution or the defence, they would be exposed to the danger either of self-crimination or falsehood. They could not have appeared with any effect on the one side without swearing to marks of violence, which would have proved their condemnation; nor on the other without witnessing to the total absence of those signs, which would have convicted them of premeditated lying. The indomitable leader had long before settled the question of their appearance, by ruling them, as he attempted to do the straightforward curator—the only person connected with the Square who came forward—to the determination of being the mutes of the tragedy; and there can be no doubt that his policy was the right one, when it was found that they not only kept themselves scathless from all but the Argive calumny, which, in their case, died away, but afterwards rose to wealth and estimation. If they were ardent students of the science of anatomy, it did not follow that they should also be ardent students of that of justice; and then self-preservation is the first duty of Nature—a keen-eyed deity, who is somewhat before her who is blind. But all these things were not weighed and computed by the dissatisfied people who were in the court that day, and they still looked for the doctors even after the Lord Advocate had begun his speech to the judges and the jury.

That speech was perhaps the best Sir William Rae had ever spoken; and it was not without its delicacies and difficulties. He knew that if the evidence of the Hares, which was, even on the face of it, a tissue of lies, were disbelieved by the jury, he had no case; and he trembled under the responsibility of satisfying an infuriated people, who, surrounding the court-house with ominous faces, made themselves heard by shouts even within the walls of the court. "I do not," he said, "present those persons, Hare and his wife, to you as unexceptionable witnesses. Assuredly they are great criminals; but the law has said that their testimony is admissible, and thus pronounced it is not undeserving of all credit. It is for you to judge of the degree of credit to which they are entitled. You saw them examined, and will draw your own conclusions. I may be prejudiced, but to me it did appear that, while the evidence of the wife was in many points exceptionable, Hare himself spoke the truth. Notwithstanding all the ability shewn in the cross-examination, I do not remember one particular in which he was led to contradict himself, or state what must be false. Doubtless there exist inconsistencies betwixt his evidence and that of his wife; but these are not of a nature that ought to induce you to withhold all credit from their testimony. Your experience will tell you how difficult it is to find two individuals who, however disposed to speak the truth, will concur in such particulars in regard to an interview which occurred at the distance of two months. But look to the situation in which these persons were placed. Look to the size of the apartment in which all this occurred. Recollect that all present were proved to have been nearly intoxicated at the time, and remember that an act of foul murder was at the time committing. Is it possible that they should not have been in a state of unusual excitement and alarm at the time? And is it wonderful that their memories should have served them differently in regard to such trifling particulars as those to which I have alluded? If they had been at one in all these points, the only just inference would have been that the story was entirely made up between them, and their evidence, in consequence, not entitled to any credit. But look to the main point of the case—the murder, and the mode in which it was done. That was a fact sufficient to rivet attention, and render sober any one, however inebriated. On this material point you find these witnesses entirely concurring,—both describing the same mode of death, and both describing a mode which corresponds completely with the appearance of the body, and which, in the opinion of the medical men, satisfactorily accounts for the death. That both Burke and Hare were participant in the foul act, no one can doubt; and I need not state to you that it matters not which was the principal aggressor in its execution. They are both art-and-part guilty."

The Dean of Faculty, for Burke, then spoke; and afterwards came Henry Cockburn, for Helen M'Dougal, with that speech, so renowned among the displays of forensic eloquence, as almost rivalling that of Jeffrey for Mrs Smith. His point of attack was—the credibility of Hare and his wife. "Our learned friend, who prosecutes here, has demonstrated by his conduct, that he is satisfied you ought not to convict without the evidence of the associates; and thus we are absolutely driven to consider what credit is due to those witnesses. If you shall agree with me in thinking that it is an absolute sporting with men's lives, and converting evidence into a mockery, to give the slightest faith to anything these persons may say, then we have the authority of the public accuser himself for holding that you must acquit. Now, on what does these witnesses' claim to credit rest? One of them is a professional body-snatcher, the other is his wife; so that, independently altogether of the present transaction, they come before you confessedly vitiated by the habits of the most corrupting and disgusting employment which it is possible to be engaged in, and one of which the chief corruption arises from its implying that he who practises it has long been accustomed to set law, feeling, and character at defiance. Then they both confess their direct accession to this particular murder—a confession which, if it had been made at the bar, would have for ever disqualified them from giving evidence in any court of justice; not having been made at the bar, they are admissible. But, since they have made the very same confession in the witness-box, their credit is as completely destroyed in the one case as it would have been in the other. Hare not only acknowledged his participation in this offence, but he admitted circumstances which aggravated even the guilt of murder. He confessed that he had sat coolly within two feet of the body of this wretched old woman while she was expiring under the slow and brutal suffering to which his associate was subjecting her. He sat there, according to his own account, about ten minutes, during which her dying agonies lasted, without raising a hand or a cry to save her. We who only hear this told, shudder, and yet we are asked to believe the man who could sit by and see it. Nor was this the only scene of the kind in which they had been engaged. The woman acknowledged that she 'had seen other tricks of this kind before.' The man was asked about his accession on other occasions, but at every question he availed himself of his privilege, and virtually confessed by declining to answer.

"But why does the law admit them? Why, just because after they are admitted it is the province of you, gentlemen, to determine how far they are to be believed. You are the absolute monarchs of their credibility. But in judging of this, do not be misled by what juries are always told of those who turn king's evidence, that they have no interest now but to speak the truth. But it is notorious that there is nobody by whom this is so universally forgotten as by those who make a bargain for saving themselves by betraying their associates. These persons almost invariably hurt the interests of their new master by the excess of their zeal in his service. They exaggerate everything, partly by the desire of vindicating themselves, and partly to merit the reward for which they have bargained. And you will observe that, in this case, these persons stand in this peculiar situation, that, so far as we know, they are still liable to be tried for similar offences. There are other two murders set forth in this very indictment, one of them committed in Hare's house, and if we may judge from what these persons say, they have been engaged in other transactions of the same kind. They came from the jail to this place to-day, and they are in jail again. Do you think that it is very improbable that when coming here they should feel that if this prosecution failed, public indignation would require another victim, and that nothing was so likely to stifle further inquiry as the conviction of those persons?

"The prosecutor seemed to think that they gave their evidence in a credible manner, and that there was nothing in their appearance, beyond what was to be expected in any great criminal, to impair the probability of their story. I entirely differ from this; and I am perfectly satisfied that so do you. A couple of such witnesses, in point of mere external manner and appearance, never did my eyes behold. Hare was a squalid wretch, in whom the habits of his disgusting trade, want, and profligacy, seem to have been long operating in order to form a monster whose will as well as his poverty will consent to the perpetration of the direst crimes. The Lord Advocate's back was to the woman, else he would not have professed to have seen nothing revolting in her appearance. I never saw a face in which the lines of profligacy were more distinctly marked. Even the miserable child in her arms, instead of casting one ray of maternal softness into her countenance, seemed at every attack (of hooping-cough) to fire her with intenser anger and impatience, till at length the infant was plainly used merely as an instrument of delaying or evading whatever question it was inconvenient for her to answer."

The Lord Justice-Clerk then charged the jury, going over the evidence, and at last directing his special attention to the case of M'Dougal:—"It is not in evidence that she took any part in the actual perpetration of the crime; but the question remains, and if answered in the affirmative, will be equally fatal to her as if she had done so, namely, whether she was an accessory, and, therefore, to be held in law as art-and-part guilty along with the other prisoner. Accession to a crime may take place before the fact as well as at the moment the crime is committing. It may likewise be *inferred* from the conduct of the party after the fact; and if you are to believe the evidence which you have heard, I am much afraid there are but too strong grounds for concluding that the female panel at the bar has been guilty of accession to the crime under investigation, whether you consider her conduct before or after the fact, or while it was perpetrating. It is impossible to conceive for one moment that, under all the circumstances of the case, the panel M'Dougal could be ignorant of the purpose for which this wretched woman Docherty was brought to the house. The state in which Burke and she appear to have lived, their brutal and dissipated habits, make it impossible to believe that either of them kept the woman in the house from the humane or charitable motives they professed to feel, and affected to shew, towards that unfortunate creature. On one occasion, it would appear, indeed, from the evidence of Gray's wife, that M'Dougal actually opposed the proposition of the woman going out of the house. The manner, too, in which she communicated the fact to Mrs Hare, that they had got a shot in the house, shews distinctly her complete knowledge of what was in view, and implicates her morally as well as legally in the guilt that afterwards ensued. Again, as to her accession during the perpetration of the crime, thus much appears, according to the evidence of Hare and his wife, that both Mrs M'Dougal and Mrs Hare were in the room, at least—whether in the bed, as Hare states, or standing between the bed and the door, as his wife swears, seems immaterial—when Burke placed himself on the body of the woman; and that upon her hearing the first screech of the woman they both flew, as Mrs Hare expresses it, to the passage, where they remained till the door was opened. By this time the crime had been accomplished, and the body thrown among the straw."

Before the jury retired, and during the time they were enclosed, Burke endeavoured to prepare the mind of M'Dougal for her fate, as, from the address of the Lord Justice-Clerk, he supposed she would be found guilty. He even gave her directions how to conduct herself, desiring her to look at and observe him when the sentence was pronounced. The jury retired at half-past eight in the morning, and after an absence of fifty minutes, returned the following verdict:—"The jury find the panel William Burke guilty of the third charge in the indictment; and find the indictment not proven against the panel Helen M'Dougal." On hearing the words of the foreman, Burke turned to M'Dougal, and coolly said, "Nelly, you are out of the scrape."

Thereafter, Lord Meadowbank proposed the sentence, prefacing at considerable length:—"Your Lordships will, I believe, in vain search through both the real and the fabulous histories of crime for anything at all approaching this cold, hypocritical, calculating, and bloody murder. Be assured, however, that I do not state this either for exciting prejudices against the individual at the bar, or for harrowing up the feelings with which, I trust, he is now impressed. But really, when a system of such a nature is thus developed, and when the actors in this system are thus exhibited, it appears to me that your Lordships are bound, for the sake of public justice, to express the feelings which you entertain of one of the most terrific and one of the most monstrous delineations of human depravity that has ever been brought under your consideration. Nor can your Lordships forget the glowing observations which were made from the bar in one of the addresses on behalf of the prisoners, upon the causes which, it is said, have in some measure led to the establishment of this atrocious system. These alone, in my humble opinion, seem to require that your Lordships should state roundly that with such matters, and with matters of science, we, sitting in such places, and deciding on such questions as that before us, have nothing to do. It is our duty to administer the law as handed down to us by our ancestors, and enacted by the legislature. But God forbid that it should ever be conceived that the claims of speculation, or the claims of science, should ever give countenance to such awful atrocities as the present, or should lead your Lordships, or the people of this country, to contemplate such crimes with apathy or indifference. With respect to the case before us, your Lordships are aware that the only sentence we can pronounce is the sentence of death."

Then the Lord Justice-Clerk, putting on the black cap, said:—"William Burke, you now stand convicted, by the verdict of a most respectable jury of your country, of the atrocious murder charged against you in this indictment, upon evidence which carried conviction to the mind of every man that heard it, in establishing your guilt in that offence. I agree so completely with my brother on my right hand, who has so fully and eloquently described the nature of your offence, that I will not occupy the time of the Court in commenting any further than by saying that one of a blacker description, more atrocious in point of cool-blooded deliberation and systematic arrangement, and where the motives were so comparatively base, never was exhibited in the annals of this or of any other court of justice. I have no intention of detaining this audience by repeating what has been so well expressed by my brother; my duty is of a different nature, for if ever it was clear beyond all possibility of a doubt that the sentence of a criminal court will be carried into execution in any case, yours is that one, and you may rest assured that you have now no other duty to perform on earth but to prepare in the most suitable manner to appear before the throne of Almighty God to answer for this crime, and for every other you have been guilty of during your life. The necessity of repressing offences of this most extraordinary and alarming description, precludes the possibility of your entertaining the slightest hope that there will be any alteration upon your sentence. In regard to your case, the only doubt that has come across my mind is, whether, to mark the sense which the Court entertains of your offence, and which the violated laws of the country entertain respecting it, your body should not be exhibited in chains, in order to deter others from the like crimes in time coming. But taking into consideration that the public eye would be offended by so dismal an exhibition, I am disposed to agree that your sentence shall be put into execution in the usual way, but unaccompanied by the statutory attendant of the punishment of the crime of murder—viz., that your body should be publicly dissected and anatomised, and I trust that if it ever is customary to preserve skeletons, yours will be preserved, in order that posterity may keep in remembrance your atrocious crimes. I would entreat you to betake yourself immediately to a thorough repentance, and to humble yourself in the sight of Almighty God. Call instantly to your aid the ministers of religion, of whatever persuasion you are; avail yourself from this hour forward of their instructions, so that you may be brought in a suitable manner urgently to implore pardon from an offended God. I need not allude to any other case than that which has occupied your attention these many hours. You are conscious in your own mind whether the other charges which were exhibited against you yesterday were such as might be established against you or not. I refer to them merely for the purpose of again recommending you to devote the few days that you are on earth to imploring forgiveness from Almighty God." The written sentence was in conformity.

Such was the sentence of Burke, sending very appropriately his body where he had sent so many others. The people were so far pleased that they had got an instalment;[14] but, in spite of the approbation bestowed on the jury by Lord Boyle, the finding of "Not proven" against Helen M'Dougal was looked upon as a mere bilking of justice. No man could have any doubt of her guilt, as being art and part, and if ever a jury acted in defiance of their consciences, it was in liberating this woman; nor do we believe that they did not think the charge proven against her—they were simply desirous that they should not afford an opportunity for the application of an old law seldom put into execution. This motive might have been looked upon as humane in an ordinary case, for assuredly the law of art and part is apt to take on cruel forms, but to withdraw Helen M'Dougal from its power was, at the very best, a squeamish and sickly humanity.

So, too, thought the public, and their anger rang through the city, even in the midst of the satisfaction universally felt at having got, at least, an instalment of justice. But were the other murderers also to get free?

THE JAIL

We may find an interest in following this unexampled criminal to the Lock-up, whither he was conveyed immediately after sentence, and where, too, M'Dougal, for the sake of safety, was placed till an opportunity was afforded of sending her away unknown to the mob. As for Hare and his wife, they behoved to continue as prisoners. No sooner had Burke been removed to the prison and placed in his separate apartment, than the old devil in him broke out. "This is a d——d cold place you have brought me till." One of the men rebuked him, but as yet it was of no use. The spirit of the man had not been touched, and as yet he lay under the gloomy weight of anger at having been betrayed, frequently bursting out in maledictions, and saying that Hare was the more guilty of the two. "He murdered the first woman," he continued. "He persuaded me to join him, and now he has murdered me; and I will regret to the last hour of my existence that he did not share the same fate." He then threw himself upon the stone bed, and lay with clenched hands, occasionally starting, as if the desire to wreak vengeance upon his betrayer had flashed through his mind, and nerved his arms to his customary assaults. While in this fit, one of the officers, not relishing the idea that he wished to excuse himself by casting even more than his share upon his colleague, made the remark, "I think I could never wish to see that man forgiven who could murder that poor, harmless, good-natured idiot, Daft Jamie," whereupon the prostrate man started, and said, "My days are numbered. I am soon to die by the hands of man. I have no more to fear, and can have no interest in telling a lie, and I declare that I am as innocent of Daft Jamie's blood as you are. He was taken into Hare's house, and murdered by him and his wife. To be sure,

180

I was guilty in so far, for I assisted to carry his body to Dr Knox, and got a share of the money." And how often do we find even the condemned, and how much more often the still successful criminal, anointing with the saliva of their own lying tongues their own ears, ay, even with the whine of self-sympathy!

As the day advanced, the perturbations produced by revenge gradually subsided, giving place to others more connected with the condition in which he now found himself, and his state of mind was attempted to be taken advantage of by the officers, always anxious to get their curiosity gratified by confessions, which they know, too, will be welcome to their superiors. But they were successful only so far that he no longer denied his guilt, even going the length of admitting a general scheme of watching poor and wretched strangers who were not likely to be inquired after by friends. Beyond this he would not go, expressing even a determination to withhold all particulars, unless counselled otherwise by his priest. Even this shewed that a great change had come over him, and shortly there was to be a still more undoubted sign, for, after remaining silent and meditative, he inquired, with an appearance of humility, and even of that politeness which was said to have formed a feature of his character at a prior period of his life, whether he would be permitted to offer up a prayer. And upon the permission having been given, this man who, only a few hours before, had exhibited the same continued impenetrability of heart manifested through the long period of his confinement, dropt upon his knees, imploring forgiveness from Almighty God for the wicked life he had led, and especially for that great crime for which he was to suffer on the gibbet; entreating, also, that his wretched partner in guilt might be brought to a full sense of her guilt—that she might repent and atone, as far as it was in her power to do so in this world, by a life of quietness, piety, and honest industry. On rising, he requested the officer to read to him a part of the Scriptures; chapter after chapter, till they amounted to six, were listened to, if not greedily accepted, with occasional remarks of the applicableness of particular passages to his crimes. Withal he had, as yet, indicated no fear—the first emotion after sentence having been revenge, and that which followed, humility and resignation, which were to remain as the prevailing condition of his mind up to the final day.

Meanwhile, the usual anxiety as to the state of the criminal's soul produced outside that conflict between the Calvinists and the Indifferents which is so common in Scotland. The one party maintained the possibility as well as the merits of the new birth, even up to the throwing away of the handkerchief; the other did not consider it either possible or probable: and while the one wished for, and waited for, the proof, the other thought, and with some reason, that so easy a way of getting quit of the consequences of the murders would not be very favourable to their non-repetition. All this Burke settled in his own Roman way, by satisfying himself that, if he wished, he could get to heaven through the ear of his confessor but there was not much evidence to shew that he entertained any strong wish on the subject, if he did not suspect that he was not a very proper person to appear in heaven. We have no wish to be irreverent, but, setting aside the old question as being inscrutable and insoluble, it is all but certain that this man never shewed a trace of that anguish of spirit under the mordacious fangs of remorse which can be accepted as the only sign of an approach to the saving faith which is in Jesus. The approvers founded upon a statement he was said to have made, that he would not accept a pardon if it had been granted. If he had been tempted by an offer, we would likely have had another tale; nor would he have been to blame, unless we are to suppose that true conversion brings along with it a predilection for being hanged, and that, while it prepares a man for death, it incapacitates him for worthily continuing in life. Independently of the total want of any signs of the real pathology of repentance, there are positive proofs that his thoughts were continually recurring to earth. He thought more of Helen M'Dougal than of a Saviour; and otherwise, we have even a ludicrous example of his sublunary grovellings. On one occasion, his mind seemed to one who was sitting by his bed to be occupied by thoughts of eternity, as he lay silent and meditative. The omen was propitious, and the pious assistant waited for the sign, which could not be less than a burst of tears, not one of which he had yet shed, or had ever been seen to shed. The sign came.

"I think," said he, with a start, "I am entitled, and ought to get that five pounds from Dr Knox which is still unpaid on the body of the woman Docherty."

"Why," replied the astonished pietist, "Dr Knox lost by the transaction, as the body was taken from him."

"That was not my business," said Burke sharply. "I delivered the subject, and he ought to have kept it."

"But you forget," said the other, "that were the money paid, Hare would have the right to a half of it."

And then came, after a little meditation, the explanation.

"I have got a tolerable pair of trousers," he continued; "and since I am to appear before the public, I should like to be *respectable*. I have not a coat and waistcoat that I can appear in, and if I got the £5 I could buy them."

But it is to be admitted that while he shewed no real signs of penitence in a Calvinistic sense,—so different these we suspect, from what are found in a votary of the confessional,—he evinced none of the dogged surliness of the hardened sinner, if his general mildness and continued politeness were not remarkable. Indeed, as we have seen, these characteristics were always, when he was not intoxicated, the prevailing features of his demeanour, from which many inferred that he purposely roused himself by large draughts of whisky to the fury which he found necessary to the perpetration of his onslaughts. This would seem to receive confirmation from the statement of a witness, who said that on these occasions he did not drink out of an ordinary measure, but used a strong-ale glass, which he would fill almost to the brim. Were this true, it would be no abatement from the malignity and sternness of the sober purpose which assuredly he must have entertained, while his external aspect was still as composed, if not as mild, as it was said to be. As a consequence of this placability, he gave way alternately to those solicitations with which he was daily pursued to utter a confession. He first made one and then another, but while these documents exhibit many discrepancies, they shew, from their curtness and desultoriness, that they were the result of a mere carelessness, only brought up to the point by pestering solicitations. Ten lines are devoted to the whole story of the murder of a human being, and if it had not been that circumstances came out on all sides, often from unknown sources, no more would have ever been known, at least as regards many of the victims, than simply that they perished. Even for these the gaping mouth of curiosity, and not less the hopeful heart of piety, was sufficiently thankful, while the hardened sceptics still refused to see the sign of the new birth.

Nor, as the short days passed to usher in the last morning, for which he said "he would not greatly weary," was there any other more signal appearance of a radical change. No doubt he received the visits of clergymen, not caring much whether of one denomination or another, and none of them were gratified with more than very ordinary manifestations of regret. There always haunted him a desire to have Hare brought to trial, yet he had art enough to place this, not to the account of revenge, but that of *humanity*. Even Burke became a philanthropist, or, what is often the same thing, could use the hackneyed words which are the fashionable tribute paid by vice to virtue. If he was not thus unable to forget the enormous debt due by his fearful associate, he was, and continued to the end to be, not less mindful of his paramour. He sent his watch and what money he possessed to her—"Poor thing, it is all I have to give to her; it will be of some use to her, and I will not need it." Yet no moisture of the eyes— the pity was only the bastard offspring of animal love.

Withal, we are frank to admit that even the breaking down

of the adamant, to the extent of confession and regret, in a man like Burke, was a triumph to religion. There is no natural way of accounting for that phenomenon of which every man is doomed to feel the experience, that while death asserts his power over the body, he extorts a contribution from the soul. Turn the question in any way you please, your final cause is nowhere, unless it be that the experience of agonised death-beds is the opportunity of virtue—a poor back-handed way of making people better, and certainly bought at a terrible expense. But even taking the advantage in this limited form, it does not exhaust the conditions of the question; for while the dying sinner is altogether unconscious that his agonies will go forth to the world and be an example, his mind is in another direction. He looks forward, and the more keenly, that he cannot look backwards. Where is the final cause now? Try again, and we suspect you will find it only in heaven.

VEJOVE

We are so apt to take signs for things, and so glibly too do the one pass into the other, that we find almost all descriptions of individuals previous to execution very much the same; and so they must needs be, for fate is the great man-tamer, and man only: the brutes merely feel the stroke when it falls—man sees it coming, knows its necessity, and therefore commits himself to resignation. Then, resignation is so grave an affair that it is often mistaken for genuine seriousness, if not for religious impression; but even here we have exceptions of men who could be merry under the gibbet or the axe—strange beings these, and more often of the virtuous than the vicious; for vice in the clutch is but a sorry affair. This doomed man, who was represented as having behaved so decently, could sing and dance the minute before he braced his cruel sinews to the work of death; and if he had been consistent, he would have acted Macpherson under the cross-beam; but the Highlander only stole cattle, while the Irishman immolated human beings, and so we find him grave and decorous because he was now to be throttled in his turn.

At four o'clock on the morning of Tuesday the 27th,—that previous to the day of execution,—he was taken off the *gad* and removed to the Lock-up in Liberton's Wynd. The reason of the early hour is evident, for the excitement of the people was such that the authorities were not satisfied that he would not be claimed by a furious mob, and dealt with as he had dealt by so many others. Notwithstanding the long period he had been in jail, there was no great change in his appearance, except a slight paleness, which, with some weakness of body, was the result of a peculiar external malady with which he had for a considerable time been afflicted;[15] nor could the sharpest observation of

186

Captain Rose, who accompanied him, detect any diminution of that composedness, or, if you please, insensibility, which had marked his demeanour all along. If there was a flutter at all, it was when he was presented with his new suit of black—either the passing feeling of the ominous dress, or satisfaction of his wish to appear respectable. In the course of the day the Catholic priests, Messrs Reid and Stewart, as well as the Protestant ministers, Messrs Marshall and Porteous, paid him a visit, and were rewarded with the usual amount of earthly regret; but with how much of remorse or faith in the Redeemer, even they could not tell, immovable as he was, and apparently unconcerned. Indeed the sole animating feeling was a desire to have the business over. "Oh, that the hour were come that is to separate me from the world!" but not a word of faith, and far less of hope. In the morning, too, when the jailer took off his heavy fetters, and they fell with a clank upon the floor,—"So may all earthly chains fall from me."

At seven, and after having experienced a sound and unbroken rest for at least five hours, Burke walked with a steady step into the keeper's room, followed by the confessor; nor yet was there any appearance of agitation or dismay. He took his seat in an arm-chair by the side of the fire, and twice or thrice arrived at that point of distress which is marked by two or three sighs. Then commenced the Catholic devotions, in which, as he had done before, he engaged with an appearance of fervour. The Protestant ministers followed up the Catholic service with some serious exhortations, in the course of which, Mr Porteous having dwelt on the words, "You must trust in the mercy of God," the doomed man exhibited symptoms of anguish; but as for anything like that "awe which is illumined by hope," he seemed to have a secret feeling that he was too deeply sunk in crime even to think of the infinite mercy of Heaven. After this portion of the exercises was gone through, he was on his way to an adjoining apartment when the executioner met and stood before him. Even this apparition, generally so fearful to a criminal when he first makes his appearance, did not dismay him. "I am not ready for you yet," was the brief salutation; and in a short time after, when he was pinioned, he bore the operation composedly, and without uttering a word. He was now asked to take a glass of wine, and having accepted the offer, he bowed to the company, and drank "Farewell to all present, and the rest of my friends." The magistrates having now gone out, returned in their robes, with their rods of office, and Burke, before going forth, expressed his gratitude to the bailies and all the other officials for the kindness and attention he had received at their hands.

Meanwhile the crowd outside had attained its greatest density. At ten o'clock on the previous night, the ceremony of setting up the scaffold had commenced. This has always been a scene in Edinburgh, but now it was a festival. The din of the workmen, and the clang of the hammers, were mingled with the shouts of the assembled people to the amount of thousands. Whenever an important part of the erection was completed in the light of the torches, up rose the cheer, as if so much had been done towards the satisfaction of their vengeance. When all was finished, and the transverse beam looked so ready for its weight, the event was honoured by three of these cheers so loud and prolonged that they were heard in Princes Street. Even the services of the workmen, always averse as they are to gallows-work, were on this occasion, and certainly never before, volunteered with emulation. By this hour, two in the morning, the closes and stairs near the spot were blocked up by masses of people, who had resolved, at the expense of so many hours' watch, to secure a good view. The inclemency of the weather drove them to any shelter that could be obtained,—in very few cases homeward,—where the morning broke upon them in gray dawn, but with the inspiration of hope. In addition to all this confusion, a constant bustle was kept up by those who, either for favour or for money,—and high prices were paid for good stances,—had procured the envied windows. After this a solemn stillness pervaded the whole scene, broken only by the splashing of the rain, which fell in torrents, accompanied with gusts of wind which whistled and moaned through the long closes.

As the morning advanced, the groups were seen hastening to their windows, and about five, the people generally began to pour in, taking their stations in front of the gallows, and upwards towards the Castlehill, while large parties of policemen and patrols successively arrived, to be posted in a strong line in front of the railing—the space left free being much larger than ordinary. Nor were the crowd on this occasion in their ordinary humour of annoying or retarding the constables in the execution of their duty, which they rather viewed as a common cause. From six to seven the concourse increased, thronging every avenue to the High Street, and hurrying in from every quarter, till the whole space, from the Tron to the Bow, threatened to be too small to hold them. Nor were the masses entirely composed of the class that usually attend such scenes. There were included, especially about the windows, not only of the dingy houses of the Lawnmarket, but also of the County Buildings, great numbers of well-dressed ladies, imparting a variety, scarcely to have been expected, to the scene, already otherwise picturesque. After seven, and when the rain, which had been excessive some hours before, began to cease, the crowd became rapidly larger still, and at eight, the entire area between the two points we have mentioned presented the aspect of an immense and closely-wedged mass of human beings, all still and watchful, never before seen there, except, perhaps, on the occasion of the King's visit. All round the scaffold you saw the crowd was composed of men—gradually outwards giving place to women, many of whom, being pressed by the dense mass around them, sent forth screams of distress; and where the pressure got less, chiefly about the circumference, the numbers of that sex were still considerable—the entire assemblage, as is the case where density is great, being moved, as it seemed, all throughout by the same impulse, coming from whatever direction. The numbers

THE STORY OF BURKE AND HARE

at this time were computed at 20,000 or 30,000. But there was one feature of this crowd which was more extraordinary than its extent or composition. In ordinary cases, at least in Scotland, there is usually manifested sympathy for the sufferer, or at least a sedate and solemn manner, as if the occasion were melancholy and instructive. All this was changed now. There was on every face an expression of something approaching to joy, as if the heart felt it was to get quit of a painful feeling of revenge, and that the relief was near. It is now eight,—St Giles's rolls forth the sounds, and every noise is stilled.

Precisely at the hour Burke was on his feet, eager to be dead, and the procession moved. He was supported by the two Catholic priests, more from the difficulty he experienced in walking with his arms so closely pinioned, than from any weakness or faltering of step. In the progress towards and up Liberton's Wynd he shewed even increased coolness and self-possession, turning from side to side in conversation, and at one part, where the ground was wet, carefully picking his steps; but at the head of the entry, where he was to get a view of the crowd, he winced, and half-closing his eyes, hurried on, as if more eager still to be out of the roar of that terrible assemblage. Nor was that roar long delayed. Upon Bailies Crichton and Small issuing from the wynd, the shout was raised in one long-continued yell, and when Burke himself was seen ascending the stair, the roar was repeated with double intensity, mixed with articulated execrations,—"Burke him!" "Choke him!" "No mercy, hangie!" Yet amidst all, Burke walked with steady step, and stood coolly below the apparatus of death. If he was much moved at all, it was to cast a look at the crowd of fierce and desperate defiance, as if he could have felt it in his heart to repeat upon every one of them his old experiment, and we suspect that he would have done it if he had had the liberty and the power.

Having taken his station in front of the drop, he kneeled with his back towards the spectators, his confessor on his right hand, and the other Catholic clergyman on the left, and repeated a form of prayer dictated by one of these reverend gentlemen. Mr Marshall, meanwhile, offered up a supplication on his behalf, the bailies and other officials joining in the devotions, with the exception of the executioner (Williams) and his assistant, who stood at the back of the drop. During all this time there was silence. On rising from his kneeling posture, Burke was observed to lift a silk handkerchief, on which his knees had rested, and put it into his pocket. There was now some hesitation in his manner, as if loath to mount; and one of the persons who assisted him to ascend, having, perhaps inadvertently, pushed him somewhat roughly to a side, that he might be placed exactly on the spot, he looked round with a withering scowl. He then *ran* up the steps, as if he hurried to death, to get beyond the reach of these terrible howls. Some further delay took place, from the circumstance of Williams, who stood behind him, endeavouring to loose his handkerchief, in which he found some difficulty. "The knot is behind," said Burke,—the only words not devotional uttered by him on the scaffold. When Williams succeeded in removing the neckcloth, he proceeded to fasten the rope round his neck, pulling it tightly, and, after adjusting and fixing it, he put upon his head a white cotton night-cap, but without pulling it over his face. While this was going on, the yells became fiercer and fiercer, mixed with the ejaculations, "Where's Hare? Hang him, too." "Don't waste rope on him." "You ——, you will see Daft Jamie in a minute." The Rev. Mr Reid then advanced, and conversed with him shortly, but earnestly, and directed him to say the Creed, which he did. As he muttered the words, his face was pale and livid, but he was still composed, unflinching, and motionless. The next act was the advance of Williams to draw the cap over his face. He manifested a repugnance to this, as if he would brave the yelling crowd even to the last extremity, and it was with some difficulty this was accomplished. Everything is now ready. He utters an ejaculation to his Maker, imploring mercy, and throws away the handkerchief with a jerk of impatience, the bolt is drawn, and Burke swings in the air amidst the deafening roar of thirty thousand people.[16] But Burke was not yet dead. He must be dead before that crowd is satisfied. From the limited length of the fall, there had been no dislocation; and for five minutes the body hung motionless, except from the impetus given by the fall, when a convulsive motion of the feet, and a general heaving, indicated a still lingering vitality. Upon observing this, the crowd raised another cheer. Twice these motions were renewed, and twice again rose the shout.

Generally, the scene of an execution is soon deserted; people give a shudder, and run away, like one who has been obliged to obey a feeling which is not pleasant, and yet is inevitable, and who enjoys a relief from the emotion. This did not occur on this occasion. The people shewed no disposition to disperse. They seemed desirous of prolonging their gratification by gloating on the ghastly spectacle, as, driven by the wind, it swung to and fro. At five minutes to nine, the bailies again came up Liberton's Wynd, still in their robes, and with their rods, and stood round the scaffold. Williams then mounted and lowered the body, and this, the last act, was celebrated by the finishing yell. The crowd then separated.

The public prints got immediately into a discussion as to the propriety of these demonstrations of feeling among a civilised people. It was by one party represented as barbarous and shocking, opposed to Christian forgiveness, and indicative of a fierce and relentless nature. The crowd was described as if made up of the *diables*, *diablesses*, and *diabletons* of the old dramas, and their cries got the name of hell-yells. There are people who, their throats being safe and their bellies well filled, look upon sin, even in its most devilish form of cruelty, as something to be dandled and conciliated into virtue like their own by sugar-plums. Those who feel no natural detestation of cruelty are not far from those that could be cruel. But supposing that these good people were as great haters of cruel men as those who shouted in the crowd, but that they felt their feeling satisfied by the arm of the law, they could only say that these people felt more satisfied than they, and that, in place of concealing their satisfaction, they expressed it openly, if you like, noisefully; and if this satisfaction must be held to be in the ratio of detestation, they were better haters of sin than those who impeached them with barbarity. So the good people get into a metaphysical net, out of which it is not very easy to get. But the question was very well settled by the *Times*, who took and shook the simperers, telling them that virtue has two sides, like everything else—one, a love for the good, and another, a hatred of what is evil, neither of which can exist without the other, and that the roused hearts of those who made the welkin ring with their roar, were just the hearts from which one might expect indications of pity for the miserable victims of that man's cruelty. It may be well for us to remember, amidst all the affected refinement of our times, that the churlishness of the honest man is the impatience of shuffling deceit and hypocrisy. When we get behind the frieze veil of the sanctuary of his affections, we often find kindness sanctified by trust,—a generosity which does not see itself, and is too often cheated by its object, and a pity, which is the more beautiful, that it wells from the stern rock of honesty and justice.

THE EXHIBITION

The earthly destiny of this marvellous man was not yet finished—the celebration of justice did not terminate by the dispersion of the thirty thousand who had assembled in the hall of the goddess Nature's own arena. They had more to do. They knew that the goddess had other forms than that in which she sends down her fiery-eyed priestess Nemesis, even that in which she despatches her moral retributions, and works them through her votaries, and that, too, wherein she is called poetical Justice, and wherein she relaxes the stern brow, and smiles with a little satire upon her beautiful lips. It is in this last form she is best loved by the imaginative; yea, and even those who, cultivating the muses, have yet a spice of humour, not inconsistent with the gravity of virtue. Had not this man sent a score of human beings to the dissecting-room? Let it be that they served the purpose of a physical science, might not he serve also the purpose of a moral cult?

During the whole of Wednesday the College was surrounded by hundreds, whose curiosity prompted them to see once more him who had immolated so many of their kind; but Dr Monro did not choose to run the risk of losing his subject, and the authorities were still afraid of a seizure, and so it was not till Thursday morning that the body was removed from the Lock-up to the dissecting-rooms of the College. At an early hour, several men dedicated to science, and among the rest Mr Liston, Mr George Combe, and his opponent Sir Wm. Hamilton, and Mr Joseph, the eminent sculptor, went to have the advantage of an examination, before the rush of the students should put that out of their power. Mr Joseph took a cast for a bust, and several amateur students gratified their curiosity by sketches. The body was that of a thick-set muscular man, with a bull-neck, great development about the upper parts, with immense thighs and calves, so full as to have the appearance of globular masses. The countenance, as we saw it, was very far from being placid, as was commonly represented, if you could not have perceived easily that there remained upon it the bitter expression of the very scorn with which he had looked upon that world which pushed him out of it, as having in his person defaced the image of his Maker.[17] Laid upon the table, the body became the subject of a lecture by the professor, and, in order to implement the sentence of the court, without so much mutilation as would interfere with the object of future inspection, the investigation was limited to the brain, laid open by removing the upper part of the cranium; the part sawed off to be subsequently replaced, so that the division could scarcely be noticed.

So far, all had proceeded in peace and with decorum; but the College was, by and by, to be the scene of a renewed excitement. About half-past two, a body of young men, consisting chiefly of students, assembled in the area, and becoming clamorous for admission, it was found necessary to send for the police,—a class of men of whose interference within the walls of the College these assertors of scholastic liberty have always shewn themselves impatient. Indignant at the opposition they had met with in the rooms, and still more angry at the conduct of the police, they made several sorties, in which they nearly succeeded in overpowering the opposition arrayed against them, at the same time that they smashed the windows at either side of the entry to the anatomical theatre. The police, finding themselves hard pressed, retreated, merely brandishing their batons; but blows received by several of them raised, in its turn, their anger, and the official weapon was used with more vigour than the magistrates, and especially the Lord Provost, who was present, seemed to relish. That dignitary accordingly got up to harangue the inflamed youths,—a liberty which could be brooked still less than the use of the batons, and amidst the cries of most opprobrious epithets, he, and along with him Bailie Small, were obliged to fly. Attempts were now made by the police to cross the square and seize prisoners; and so far they succeeded, but it was only to be left to witness the captured *élèves* reclaimed, and carried off amidst shouts of triumph. Even some, whom the police got conveyed to Dr Monro's rooms, were searched for, and pulled out into liberty, adding, in their turn, to the shouts of the liberators. It was then attempted to make a dash, and clear the area of the assembled collegians by a promiscuous pell-mell, but the police again found themselves overmatched, and could not even retain their own ground in the open area. The contest was renewed more than once with varying success, and no man could tell how long the battle would last, as time, in place of moderating the passion of the students, served only to increase it, and every sortie and shout threatened some issue involving life. One or two of the police were carried off wounded, amidst cries of victory, and the battle, which had now lasted from half-past two to four, threatened even worse consequences than had yet resulted, when the professors got alarmed. Dr Christison at length made his appearance with the olive, and intimated to the youths that he had made arrangements whereby they would be admitted to see the body of Burke in fifties, giving his personal guarantee for their good conduct.

This intimation, which was in fact a victory,—achieved, too, with a compliment to their honour,—was received with loud cheers of "Hurrah for Christison!" and "Burke's our own!" and presently all their fury subsided amidst the returning hilarity of loud laughter. But matters were not at all satisfactory outside in the street. The people had been restless all day. The sight of the hanging, in place of allaying their passion against Burke, seemed to have inflamed them into a desire to gloat their eyes on his remains; and many intimated their design, in the event of being defeated, of forcing an entry into the anatomical theatre, and dragging the body out, to tear it in pieces. To this, the news of the success of the students inflamed them the more, but as it was now getting dark, and several scouts sent among them by the authorities having circulated the report that the magistrates and Dr Monro would make arrangements for general admission to the anatomical theatre next day, the crowd began to separate, but each carrying away the determination, which they growled out as they went, that unless the terms were adhered to, their purpose would be executed on the morrow.

On Friday the arrangements were made for a grand public exhibition. The body of the hanged man was placed on the black marble table of the theatre, so as to be seen by the visitors as they passed from one door to another, from which they could get exit in another direction. The news meanwhile had spread through both the Old and New Towns that the body of Burke was to be seen by all and sundry, and the commotion throughout all ranks, high and low, was only equalled by that of the day of execution. The Old Town presented the appearance of a holiday. Thousands took their way to the College, where they found the doors open and the exhibition begun, but as the stream of entrants was necessarily narrow, and of slow movement, the street and the area inside soon presented an appearance scarcely less crowded than on the day previous. The programme was very soon understood, and was indeed so simple and easily wrought, however tedious as regards time, that the people had only to try to get into the moving stream when they were pushed forward quietly and orderly enough to the envied scene. There on the table lay the victim naked, with the part of the scull which had been sawed off so artistically restored that the mark of the junction could scarcely be observed. The spectacle was sufficiently ghastly to gratify the most epicurean appetite for horrors. There was as yet no sign of corruption, so that the death pallor, as it contrasted with the black marble table, shewed strongly to the inquiring and often revolting eye; but the face had become more blue, and the shaved head, with marks of blood not entirely wiped off, rather gave effect to the grin into which the features had settled at the moment of death. However

197

inviting to lovers of this kind of the picturesque the broad chest that had lain with deadly pressure on so many victims—the large thighs and round calves, indicating so much power—it was the face, embodying a petrified scowl, and the wide-staring eyes, so fixed and spectre-like, to which the attention was chiefly directed.

As the stream moved on with recurring pauses, when some, more intent than others, held back to have a moment or two's more time, it was curious to view the ever-varying emotions of the spectators. Many were there who could not in any other circumstances have looked upon a corpse at all, and you might have seen some half-irresolute adventurers who, as they neared, feared the sight, and would have backed out but that they were compelled to proceed, when the unsteady eye, anxious to avert itself, was caught by the horrible charm and fixed. No one, so far as we could see, however nervous, either shut the eyes or turned them away altogether; nor could you detect a single trace of pity—the prevailing expression, a malign satisfaction, strangely and staringly returned, as it were, by the grin of the corpse, which had the advantage of eternal persistency. Extraordinary as all this moving scene was,—and certainly nothing of the kind had ever been witnessed in Edinburgh before,—it was rendered more so by the occurrence among the close stream of a few women, amounting in all, we understood, to seven or eight, who, having made their way up-stairs, not perhaps with the intention of going altogether forward, were moved on and could not escape. The caught virgins, true to their nature, struggled so well in the net of their curiosity, that you would have said they were really anxious to get back, and yet somehow their struggles seemed unaccountably rather to help them on; but at any rate it was certain they were modest, and shrank at the thought of the coming sight, for they held down their heads to avoid the stare of the men, and when they arrived at the point, only looked with a squint, sufficient at once for entire gratification as well as for immunity from the charge of not being feminine and delicate. It is doubtful, notwithstanding, however influenced by the sense of the *nil dulcius quam omnia scire*, whether they would venture again upon such another Junonian venture; for the males, who reserve to themselves the exclusive right of witnessing such spectacles, bestowed on them such and so many tokens of indignation as might have cured them for ever of their original sin.

The numbers who supplied this continued stream may be judged of when it is mentioned that by actual enumeration it was found that upwards of sixty per minute passed the corpse. This continued from ten in the morning till darkening, and as the crowd, when we saw it at three o'clock, was still increasing, as one told another of what he had seen, we cannot compute the numbers at less than twenty-five thousand persons; add to this those who had a private interview, and we arrive again at the number present at the execution, thirty thousand—a greater number than ever visited royalty lying in state, at least within the kingdom of Scotland. Nor did the entire day suffice for the satisfaction of this curiosity. As many were ready for the following day; but, to the disappointment of these, it was announced that all further ingress would be denied. Next day, Saturday, the front of the College again presented a scene of confusion. Another crowd had collected—growling at the conduct of the officials—crying for the opening of the anatomical theatre; and long after they had ascertained that no further exhibition would be permitted, the people stood and continued to gaze at the College walls, till, exhausted of their patience, they reluctantly departed, leaving fresh arrivals, which continued during the entire day to occupy their places.[18]

One might have thought that the excitement, at least in so far as regarded Burke—for the other culprits were a precious reserve, whose fortunes might fill a volume of great interest—would have thus ended; but at that time the science of phrenology was in its zenith, the Combe-and-Hamilton controversy in full vigour; and so, next came the battle of the phrenologists and the old Scotch school of mental philosophers. Burke's head, so ingenious in devising a new species of murder, which should bear his immortal name, as well as in discovering a new estimate of the value of the human body, was measured and mapped into philoprogenitiveness, veneration, destructiveness, and all the rest, so as to be in all time coming the example and test of the character possessed by the genuine *à priori* and *à posteriori* murderer. And it was a solemn occasion. The measurements were recorded and published. The accuracy of the mere figures was not denied, but the inferences were disputed with such acrimony that the scientific battle commenced. Everywhere there was a measuring of craniums, and even wise people, who never had any doubt of the smallness of their destructiveness, were startled into the conviction that they required not only to take care of themselves, but to be taken care of by others. Mr Combe bade fair to be the only man who was to be benefited by the labours of Burke. A considerable number of people, who were not sure of their harmlessness, notwithstanding they were very timid, and to others and themselves very innocent, waited upon him to ascertain what they in reality were; and if you had stood at his door, you might have judged by the faces of his consultors how much they were above or below the fatal 6·125— the most marvellous bump that had ever been seen on the head of man since the days of that great man-killer Hercules. It was in vain that the Hamiltonians brought forward the measurements of men scarcely less famous in their philanthropic way than Howard. The great development of destructiveness had in their cases been accompanied by *inactivity*, and the examples went for nought; and so, in like manner, the examples of other murderers who could not boast of more than 5·4, were satisfactorily set aside for the reason of *activity*. The Hamiltonians pushed their advantage, and demanded a return to the old doctrines and common sense; but the Combeans would not admit the demand. The frying-pan sued for could not be returned or paid for—1st, Because it was an old one with holes in it; 2dly, Because it was returned long before; and, 3dly, Because it was never borrowed. If one thing won't do, another will: if you drive us out of size, we fall back upon activity; if from activity, we flee to size. Burke, in addition to all his other achievements, thus killed a science. Having wrought so assiduously for anatomy, he ended by burking phrenology.

THE
PROSECUTION
AGAINST HARE

The public had got only an instalment; and the fingering of the money produced only desire for more, to make up the debt to justice. Whatever might become of the women, Hare must be hanged, dissected, and exhibited in the same way as Burke, otherwise the peace of the city would be again in jeopardy. He was the greater criminal of the two, and the people had no moral vision to comprehend how the Lord Advocate could bargain with, and feel himself bound to keep honour with, one who, having lost the form and features of the sacred "image," was beyond the pale of humanity. You don't think of the moral obligation to refrain from killing a tiger merely because he left in your way another cruel animal, which, for want of a lamb eaten by the more rapacious, you found it convenient to dine off.

After his examination, and when the officers were removing Hare from the court-house to the Calton Jail, they were struck with dismay to find that he had been seized with a fit of glee, which, for want of an epithet derived from humanity, we may term diabolical; but the officers were simple, and so was he: they should have known the man, and he knew himself—a creature in whom there being no good to produce the variety which constitutes character, there could be nothing but pure and unmixed evil. If the devil is not a simpleton,—father of lies and master of devices as he is,—it is just because having once known the good he could hate it. Hare never knew even that, and could not be said to hate what he could not understand. Yet he laughed, not heartily, that would be a misnomer, but hepatically, from the liver, because he fancied that he had escaped from justice at the expense of the life of his accomplice. The public, much as they cried for his blood, were simple too, in so far as they believed that while in jail he shunned the public gaze, and muffled himself up in the bed-clothes when visited by the authorities; whereas the man, instead of thinking he had done anything shameful or even wrong, was rather proud of his ingenuity, not only amusing himself in the public ground attached to the ward, but exhibiting rather satisfaction at being looked at.[19] Nor, while in the very height of his effrontery, did he construe the marked dislike of the prisoners, every one of whom shrank from his touch or even approach, into anything short of spite because he was now free—being only there as under the protection of the authorities—and his companions poor bond devils. So far we may believe; but there might have been a small tax on the credulity of the time, when it was believed that he construed in the same way the conduct of those companions when, upon the occasion of there being more onlookers from without than the shame of the jail-birds relished, they were in the habit of hitching him forward as a great spectacle, by the attraction of whom their merely comparative merits might be overlooked.

By and by, as the vengeful feeling of the public against the man increased, and nothing for a time was heard but the stifled groans for the second victim, it came out that the public prosecutor, having procured Hare's co-operation as a *socius criminis* to convict Burke, and all the information which was necessary to bring home to the latter the three charges in the indictment, the Crown was pledged in honour not to proceed against him on any one of these counts. This was, in effect, to say that he was free whenever he could get out of the hands of the infuriated people; because, in so far as regarded the other cases, there was no evidence independently of his, and he would take precious care to withhold every word to criminate himself. It is needless to say that the most sensible of the editors, and all the thinking and honourable of the people, considered this statement of the authorities as reasonable and proper. They would stand upon the honour of the Crown and the dignity of human nature, even at the expense of giving liberation to a man who, by his own confession, was a murderer. They would therefore leave the vulgar to the *charum lumen* of their prejudices, and so they were left. But, while thus taking this high and dignified ground against those whom a natural hatred of atrocity was said to make low, some ingenious one of their ranks struck out the idea that, though the Crown was shut up to let Hare off, some relative of one of the murdered persons might prosecute for assythment, or a compensation for the loss of life; and immediately it was found that Daft Jamie's mother, Mrs Wilson, with his sister, Janet Wilson, would be willing, if not anxious, to take the post of prosecutor—a piece of intelligence which pleased the public wondrously.

This proposition was brought to bear by an application presented to the Sheriff on the part of the Wilsons, praying for liberty to precognosce witnesses with a view to the prosecution of Hare; on the deliverance upon which progress was being rapidly made in the examination of several persons, when immediately there was presented to his lordship a petition for Hare, craving to be set at liberty. On the 21st of January, the Sheriff pronounced an interlocutor refusing the prayer of Hare's petition, on the ground that there was no decision finding that the right of the private party to prosecute is barred by any guarantee or promise of indemnity given by the public prosecutor; but, in consequence of the novelty of the case, he superseded further progress with the precognitions, in order that Hare might have an opportunity of applying to the Court of Justiciary.

This judgment was accordingly brought under review of the High Court by what is technically called a bill of advocation, suspension, and liberation—the meaning of which is simply that Hare tried another chance for freedom by applying to the highest tribunal. The Lord Justice-Clerk, who saw at once that the question was so far new, and of the first importance, not only in its merits, but viewed in relation to the state of the public mind, wished to have it judged of by all the Lords, and he therefore called upon the public prosecutor to answer the request of Hare. The Lord Advocate, who, no doubt, felt himself placed in a delicate position, but still determined to stand by the law and the dignity of the Crown, accordingly presented his answer; and long pleadings, called informations, having been lodged, the case came to be tried before the Court on the 2d February. The celebrated Jeffrey appeared for Mrs Wilson, and Duncan M'Neill for Hare. It was maintained on the part of Hare, said Mr Jeffrey, that the public prosecutor was entitled to make a compact, to which compact their Lordships were bound to give effect; that their Lordships had no discretion, but that it rested entirely with the Lord Advocate to enter into such compact, and to extend immunity to any number of cases, without the control of the judge; in short, that the Lord Advocate possessed the uncontrolled power of exercising the royal prerogative. And this he might do, not merely in respect of the particular crime as to which a *socius criminis* was to be used as a witness, but might, if he chose, extend it to all other crimes of which he might have been guilty. Whenever the Lord Advocate stipulated an immunity, it seemed to be maintained, on the other side, that a sufferer by housebreaking, fire-raising, and other crimes, was to be deprived of his right, as a private party, to prosecute the guilty perpetrator of the wrong, and that the Lord Advocate had a power to enter into a compact by which he could grant immunity for offences, past or future, known or unknown. Such a prerogative would be to invest the public prosecutor with a power of pardon which only belonged to the Crown, and this, too, without a tittle of authority, amounting to an assumption of the authority of Parliament; and so forth. But all the eloquence of Jeffrey would not do. The judges had, long before this day of judgment, been down in the deep wells of authority, and, as one of the enraged people said, came up drunk with law, and kicked sober justice out of court. Certainly, if such a profane expression could be used, these learned men might have been in that state, for seldom had they appeared so surcharged with authorities. They seem to have rummaged every corner of the Advocates' Library and the Register-Office to find out the origin of the law of king's evidence, and to have hunted out every decision bearing upon the case, so that, it would seem, Hare should be rendered as famous for settling a great and hitherto doubtful point of law, as Burke was destined to be for putting an end to a science. After all, the judges who decided for Hare were found to be right; and, indeed, any one looking at the subject, could not fail to see that, as the Lord Advocate represented the king, and the king, as the great public protector of his subjects and prosecutor of their wrongs, represented his people, and Mrs Janet Wilson and her daughter among the rest, the immunity promised by his lordship to Hare really included an immunity implied as given by Mrs Wilson and her daughter.

While the case was going on, and Hare anxious to get out, he founded his hope on an extraordinary delusion, which could have occurred to nobody but himself. He understood well enough the meaning of the long word assythment, and asked his agent, with one of his leers, what was the value of Daft Jamie. The price given by the doctors, he said, was too much, because, if he had been offered alive to any one, he would not have been bought at any price, so that his mother had no claim, and the judges were just trifling away both their time and their brains about a thing of no value. Incredible as this may seem,—and doubtless many reports passed that were not true,—it is not unlike the man; for it never was asserted, by those who had access to him, that he had the slightest notion of having done anything that was wrong. He was, indeed, one of those men, not so uncommon as the optimists may think, or so impossible as the Christian philosophers maintain, whose consciences are entirely turned round about, and who, when they come to think seriously, find the worm gnawing on the wrong side. Their pain is for any good they may have been tempted to do, their relief for any evil they have been fortunate enough to perpetrate, so true is it that nature is jealous of man's having it in his power to say that any proposition is absolutely true, and without an exception. But such phenomena, which, after all, are so uncommon as to deserve the name of monstrosities, need not flutter the faith of such men as Chalmers, who found upon the universality of the law of conscience as proving the goodness, if not also the existence, of God. It is only a matter of curiosity that, while such advocates recognise and explain alone the exceptional cases, where there is simply a *want* of the faculty, they do not seem to think that there can occur, or ever could have occurred, a case where its decrees are absolutely reversed. But, after all, we have to keep in view that the whole conditions, even of Hare's nature, were not exhausted. For aught we know, if he had been condemned to die, Providence would have vindicated her rule even as to him, and the faculty been observed to right itself. Hare was, at any rate, declared at liberty.

THE HUNT OUT

We take up the end of the thread of our last chapter, and say, that as the potential developments of a man's heart cannot be exhausted except by death, we cannot pronounce, until that issue arrives, of God's purpose with him. We have known many men who, by a redundancy of the oil of self-satisfaction, have kept the lamp of jovial humour, or light recklessness, or flippant egotism, burning for a long period of years, and indulging all the while in the boast of an indomitable persistiveness. There are many such, but we suspect they are generally mere actors; and we are the more satisfied of the hollowness of their pretensions when we learn the account of them from those who have access to their privacy, and are apt to verify the saying that, as no man is a hero to his valet, so no jolly fellow, *pococurante*, or devil-darer is always such to his wife, children, servants, or friends. Even were it so, we would still say that the conditions have not been exhausted by some calamity which *may* come, or by death, who *must* come; and as there are worse evils than even death, the power of holding out is only an inverse mode of expressing the power of what is held out against. These remarks occur to us as we are now to follow the fortunes of the remaining three of the quaternity.

Hare was still Hare up to the hour of his freedom, and that freedom, for which he had sacrificed the life of the man whom he had taught the trade of murder, was to be the test to try his obduracy, and prove the ruin of that persistency in evil which had mocked the ghosts of a score of murdered beings. He was let loose only to flee, and to flee under the only terror he felt—the uplifted hands of an avenging people. At a little past eight on the Thursday night, after the decision of the High Court of

Justiciary, he was relieved from his cell in the Calton Hill Jail. It was a night of bitter frost, just such a one as Vejove would select for sending a Cain-marked murderer out upon the world. After being muffled up in an old camlet cloak, he walked, in company with the head turnkey, as far as the Post-office in Waterloo Bridge without meeting with the slightest molestation. At this point his companion called a coach, and conveyed him to Newington, where the two waited till the mail came up. The guard's edition of the story varies thus far, that he took up an unknown passenger in Nicolson Street, where he was ordered to blow the horn. But the difference is immaterial, and might easily arise from Hare's state of mind. Be this as it may, he got safely seated on the top of the coach without challenge and without suspicion. In the way-bill he figured as a Mr Black— not an inappropriate name—and the tall man who came to see him off, exclaimed, when the guard cried, "All's right," "Good-bye, Mr Black, and I wish you well home."[20] At Noble-house, the second stage on the Edinburgh road, twenty minutes were allowed for supper; and when the inside passengers alighted and went into the inn, Hare was infatuated enough to follow their example. At first he sat down near the door, behind their backs, with his hat on, and his cloak closely muffled about him. But this backwardness was ascribed to his modesty, and one of the passengers, by way of encouraging him, asked if he was not perishing with cold. Hare replied in the affirmative, and then, moving forward, took off his hat, and commenced toasting his paws at the fire—a piece of indiscretion which can only be accounted for by his characteristic recklessness, not yet cured; and little, indeed, was he aware that Mr Sandford, advocate, one of the counsel employed against him in the prosecution at the instance of Daft Jamie's relations was then standing almost at his elbow. A single glance served all the purpose of the fullest recognition, and, as Hare naively enough remarked, "He shook his head at me," somewhat after the fashion, we suppose, of the ghost in Macbeth.

On the horn being blown, he contrived, after the manner of the Greek slayer, who was always ahead of the three Furies, to be first at the coach door, and finding an empty seat inside, he actually occupied it. "Take that fellow out," cried the indignant counsel, and out accordingly he was taken, and transferred to the top, whereupon Mr Sandford, eager, perhaps, to justify what had the appearance of cruelty on so bitter a night, revealed to his fellow-travellers what, perhaps, he ought not to have done. A secret is like gas, it spreads without burning, and at Beattock, the guard as well as the driver, knew all. They were only obliged to conceal it because there was no one to tell it to; but on the arrival of the coach at Dumfries, the servants who attended to take the inside passengers' luggage, got the hint, and the news flew like a fire-flaught. Meanwhile, Hare had slunk into the coach-office of the King's Arms. People were seen hurrying thither from every direction, crying, "Hare's in the King's Arms!" By eight o'clock, a large crowd had collected, and by ten it was perfectly overwhelming. You might have walked over the heads of a mass of people in the High Street and Buccleuch Street, amounting to 8000, reminding us of a great fair, when the country empties itself into the town. Their object they did not tell, nor was it necessary, except in so far as having known that he was for Port-Patrick, they proposed to do the great man honour *in their own way.* If Hare had got among these people, he would assuredly have been sacrificed, for the dissatisfaction at his release was not confined to the metropolis. Meantime, the man, considering himself safe inside, and having from the first been surrounded by a knot of coachmen and guards, who handed him part of their ale, he clattered away, drinking absurd toasts, such as "Bad luck to bad fortune," and not denying his identity: "No use for that now;" but all questions about his crimes he evaded; "he had said enough before;" "he had done his duty in Edinburgh." Yet we suspect that the light talk was the effect of the ale, for, to a gentleman who visited him, with a view to know something of his early history, he complained that he had no money, and when a guinea was handed to him, "he burst into tears." Yes, the time had come, or was approaching, when the hitherto maintained conditions of insensibility were to be broken, not for penitence, not even for remorse, but for regret, if not despair.

When this visitor retired, the people forced the door, and in an instant Hare was squeezed into a corner, reminding one of a hunted fox when, getting into a *cul de sac*, he turns round, shews his teeth, and vainly attempts to keep the jowlers at bay. In the absence of the police, his situation was far from being free from peril. The torrent of imprecations was fearful, and "Burke him!" came so savagely from so many throats, that he seemed on the very eve of being laid hold of and torn asunder. It is reported that one old woman was not only wonderfully emphatic and ferocious in her gestures, but strove to get forward to strike "the villain" with the end of her umbrella. And lucky it was that she did not get in the front, for mischief, like fire, needs only a beginning, and if one individual had lifted a hand, his fate would have been sealed. When the police arrived, the room was cleared, and Hare conveyed to a safer place till the Galway mail should start. With a view to this the inn-yard was closed with difficulty, the horses put too, and the coach brought out. But the mob, with rather more eyes than the old watcher, had previously taken their plans, as if by instinct, and their aspect appeared so threatening that it was impossible to drive the mail along the High Street with the "fearful man" either inside or out. The coach accordingly started perfectly empty, two passengers having been sent forward a few miles in a gig. The crowd opened and recoiled—the tremendous rush, the appalling waves on waves of people, heaving to and fro; and now the coach is again surrounded, amidst yells the doors opened, the interior exposed, even the boot examined. The people were still more exasperated because their plan was defeated—no other than to stop the mail at the middle of the bridge, and precipitate Hare from the parapet down into the river. Failing in this, they had determined to waylay the coach at Cassylands toll-bar, and there execute their purpose in another way, and as a preparation they had forcibly barricaded the gates. The crowd now rolled back in one continuous wave; and when the fact became known that he was still in the room of the inn, he was again broken in upon, forced to sit and stand in all positions and postures, turned round and back again, so that cool, insensate, and apathetic as he was, he was now stimulated into terror. Amidst all this the imprecations were repeated, and another woman, after having exhausted her ingenuity in words, seized him by the collar, and tugged so manfully that he was nearly strangled. At one moment the voice of a sturdy ostler got ascendancy over the noise:— "Whaur are ye gaun, man? or whaur can ye gang to? Hell's ower gude for ye. The very deevils, for fear o' mischief, wadna daur to let ye in; and as for heaven, that's entirely oot o' the question." Others, who wanted to drive matters to extremity, pretended to take his part, and urged him on. The old spirit came again, and he called out, "to come on, and give him fair play;" but this was a spurt, for despair was extending over him her dark wings, and so crucified was he, that he started, took his bundle, determined to "let the mob tak their will o' him"—a resolution in which he was checked by a medical man.

The innkeeper, Mr Fraser, in the meantime, apprehensive for the safety of his premises, was anxious to eject his dangerous customer. The entire town was, in short, so completely convulsed that it was impossible to tell what would happen next, and, after deliberation, the magistrates, who had a very onerous duty to perform, hit upon an expedient for getting quit of him, which, though successfully executed, had ten chances to one against it. Betwixt two and three, a chaise and pair were brought to the door of the King's Arms, a trunk buckled on, and a great fuss made; and while these means were employed as a decoy-duck, another chaise was got ready almost at the bottom of the back entry, and completely excluded from the view of the mob. The next step was to clear the room, and, after this, to get Hare to clamber, or, rather, jump out of the window of his prison, and crouch, cat-like, along the wall facing the stables. The task was well executed: the moment he got to the bottom and sprang into the chaise, the doors were closed and the whip cracked. Never before did a chaise rattle so furiously along the streets of Dumfries. To pass Mr Rankin's and round the corner of Richardson's brewery occupied only moments; but here the turn was taken so sharply that the chaise ran for a time on two side wheels. Had it upset, Hare was doomed; but the driver recovered the position of the coach, and away again at even a more rapid rate. The mob by this time had become suspicious of a manoeuvre, and, as the driver had a considerable round to make, they rushed in a twinkling and in prodigious masses to intercept him at the middle of the sands. A rush down Bank Street like the letting out of waters, and from the opposite side of the river, numbers, suspecting the cause, hurried with such fury over the old bridge that the driver seemed destined to be outflanked and surrounded; nor could he have avoided this had it not been for the mettle of his horses and the willing arm that urged them on. Once again his charge is saved from instant death.

Even yet the flight was far from being accomplished. At every instant, he was intercepted and threatened, and, though he cowered down, stones threatened him on every side. Some stood still from inability to run, but others immediately supplied their places, filling up with almost the speed of thought the wake of the careering coach. An impression now prevailed that the driver meant to gallop out the Galloway road, and a rush was made to the western angle of the new bridge—a mistake which operated as a diversion in favour of the driver—nor were the few moments gained misemployed. The sharp corner of Dr Wood's laboratory was cleared almost at a single bound, and as he had now a broad street before him, nothing could exceed the fury with which he drove up to the jail door. Mr Hunter had previously received his cue, and, though a strong chain was placed behind the door, an opening was left to admit the fugitive. A spring over the gulf, and Hare is again safe.

His escape enraged the mob still more. As the numbers increased, they laid regular siege to the place of safety, preventing all ingress or egress. From four to eight, all was clamour and execration, and at nightfall, for reasons of their own, they smashed and extinguished the neighbouring lamps. A ponderous piece of iron was used as a battering-ram, aided by heavy stones, the rebound of which was so incessant and long-continued, that every fear was entertained they would succeed in forcing the jail. It was next proposed to apply tar barrels and peats for the purpose of forcing the door. By this time the magistrates were thoroughly roused. The militia staff and police had done their best without avail, and it was not till one hundred special constables were sworn in and marched to the spot, with batons, that the peace of the city was restored. Still the streets were in commotion, and it was afterwards ascertained that the mob still retained the intention of forcing the prison; but as the night waxed, their resolution waned, and at one o'clock on Saturday morning not an individual was seen in Buccleuch Street. As the opportunity was too good to be lost, Hare was roused from his bed, where he had so long shivered, and ordered to prepare. While putting on his clothes, he trembled violently, yet inquired eagerly for his cloak and bundle; but as these articles were not at hand, he was told he must go without them. As the whole population of Galloway were in arms, and as the mail had been surrounded and searched at Crocketford toll-bar, and probably at every other stage betwixt Dumfries and Port-Patrick, it would have been madness to send him across the bridge, and he was recommended to take another route. At three o'clock he was seen by a boy passing Dedbeck, and must have been beyond the border by the break of day. The driver of the mail reported that he saw him at a quarter-past five sitting on a heap of stones within two miles of Carlisle. It seems he had been again recognised, and told that the people of Carlisle were prepared to kill him; and although he appeared completely done up, he turned by the Newcastle road, and doubtless made his bed in the open fields. Little more was ever heard of Hare. If the Almighty, as Mr M'Diarmid added, when He appeared specially in the affairs of the world, left Cain to wander hopeless on the face of the earth, why should not Hare have been subjected to the same species of punishment? and, without wishing to refine too far, we may say, as the Roman said long ago, "Everything must bow to the majesty of the law; and that, from the weightiest circumstance down to the smallest, there is a medium course—a middle path—beyond which no rectitude and no safety to mortals can exist."

As for Mrs Hare, she was liberated as soon after the trial as safety would permit; but almost immediately upon her release, a crowd collected round her. It was a cold, snowy day. She was pelted with snow-balls and stones, and had some commiseration not been felt for the child she carried, she would, in all probability, have fallen a victim to the violence of the mob. Rescued by the police, she was conveyed to the Police-office, where she found shelter and protection. She afterwards escaped, and wandered about the country, not knowing whither to betake herself. At length she turned up in Glasgow, in the hope of getting a steamer for Ireland. For this purpose she was obliged to wait, and at night she ventured out to the Broomielaw to get information. Next morning she repeated her venture, and in Clyde Street was recognised by a woman, who cried out, "Hare's wife—Burke her!" and threw a large stone at her. The signal was enough. A crowd soon gathered, and pursuing her into the Calton offered her every indignity, nor can it be known how far they would have proceeded if she had not been taken from their hands by the police. It was described as truly pitiful to see her stretched on the guard bed of the cell, with her child clasped to her breast, weeping bitterly, and imploring the officers not to allow her to be made a show of. She was entirely ignorant of the fate of Hare, with whom she said she would never live again. All she wanted was to get to Ireland, and end her miserable life in some retired part of the country with penitence. She afterwards left Glasgow in the Fingal, and nothing more was ever heard of Mrs Hare.[21]

Some traces were also got of Helen M'Dougal.[22] Upon her release from the lock-up house, she had the audacity or folly to repair to her old haunts in the West Port, and even to appear in the street. She was recognised in an instant, and at once surrounded by a mob threatening to seize her, but fortunately the proximity of the district office insured protection, and with difficulty she was lodged. Yet this was only the sign for an uproar. The mob increased to an alarming size for the slender force, and the officers were obliged to resort to an expedient to prevent an assault. A ladder was placed at a back window, by which it was pretended that she had got down, and the mob having dispersed, probably to pursue her, she was conveyed, under an escort, to the head-office. Again venturing out, she was repeatedly exposed to similar dangers, till, finding it impossible to put out her head in Edinburgh, she left secretly for Redding in Stirlingshire. She afterwards left that village, no doubt to be a wanderer, like the others, and with as little hope of rest to her feet as of peace to her soul.

THE FINAL CAUSE

There are one or two considerations connected with the history we have given which, though having something of a philosophical look, are yet sufficiently practical to be appreciated by the ordinary observer of human nature and the ways of God with His creatures. It is doubtful if, from the beginning, the actors in this drama were ever sufficiently understood; if it is not more true to say, that the people, eager to conserve the prestige of man's dignity, have been inclined, after the manner of purists, to set off exceptions to the general laws of human nature as the foil of some heaven-born exemption from crime. They have uniformly mixed contempt with their hatred of these strange men. They have not thought them entitled to be objects of consideration, far less study. They have represented them as something so far below their kind, that their deeds can no more enter as elements into a lesson than those of maniacs, or of the lower animals, who are exempted from the laws of responsibility, and so they have shewn an inclination to cast them out of the wide province of history; or, if they would allow them to remain within the precincts of annals, they would consign them to the grotesque page of *monstra horrenda*.

It is no doubt beneficial for man to think well of the good, but it is not advantageous for him to think lightly of the evil potentialities of his nature. We cannot deny that these men and women were sane; and we have higher authority than a wish-born logic or a self-gratifying rhetoric to satisfy us that "the heart of man is deceitful above all things and desperately wicked." The authority is from heaven, and there is no want of verifying examples upon earth; nay, if we abate the "putrid coruscations," or what have been called "the blue lights of

217

necromancy" that play round these sordid murders, and which are at least nourished by the fancy, we may find every day cases scarcely less cruel and scarcely less sordid,—if we might not even say that it requires some analysis to find the difference in mere turpitude between a man who murders for the money that is about the body and one who slays for that which the body will bring. Then the repetition adds nothing to the atrocity of the individual act, while the premeditation is as signal in the slouching highwayman as in him who wiles the victim to the fatal den. In short, we may make what parade we please of the gradations of atrocity and the shades of our feelings, but we must always come back to the beginning, that there are no degrees of wickedness in those who have renounced God.

Not only, however, were these individuals sane; one among them, and the leader, was intelligent, had wit and humour, could feel the superficial sentiment of a pathetic lyric, and, above all, possessed ingenuity to the extent of inventing a new crime which has gone, with his name, over the world. The women, too, were intelligent and apt; nor has it been said that Mrs Hare did not feel the yearnings of a mother, or that M'Dougal was false to the affection, however low, which bound her to the tyrant who enslaved her. Even Hare was not a fool—a character inconsistent with a will-power which could govern a woman of his wife's acknowledged adroitness, and lead, if not rule, a man such as Burke, so that we may say that, so far as regards mere intelligence, the quaternity were a fair enough specimen of the people of their class, in which certain parts of our city abound; while Burke may be safely pronounced as being considerably above the average of uncultivated minds, left as a waste for the culture of the devil. But not only in this aspect were they worthy of study—they were perfect in their moral organisation as embodiments of evil, with no scruples, no misgivings, no backcomings of penitence, no fear of the future, and no remorse for the past. They were not only "clear grits"—they were "crystals." They were, out of millions, creatures suited to the work they did—the work was suited to them, and they did it with all that concentration of purpose and uniformity of action which proclaim the being under alienation from the Almighty.

In what we here venture to say we have a sufficient apology for disinterring these people and their deeds, as constituting the great lesson, that it is the *occasion* that tests the man; even as it is true what the proverb says, that a man is never known till he is invested with power. As an abstract aphorism, that proverb has but little influence; it is only when we see it reduced to the concrete that we feel its truth and lay it up in our hearts; and this we are the more ready to do that, while we are well penetrated by that horror which is fear, we are not the less under the influence of that other horror, which is hatred. And here we insist for a distinction which may silence those who indulge in the fancy, that it is not useful or good to pander to an appetite for details which, while they harrow the heart, are yet, by some strange peculiarity in our nature, not without a grim charm calculated to fascinate and yet not to deter. The fault here lies at the door of the chronicler, for it is he who holds the wand, and it requires only the mode of using it to change the appetite into a revulsion, and to make the horror which is hatred paramount for good. It is only man who is false to nature, never nature to herself. Such deeds she exhibits in their true colours, and he who interprets her can only be true to his office when he produces those emotions which she produced in him uncoloured by the lights of a factitious fancy.

We may thus, even without going further, find a final cause in these terrible acts done by creatures made after the image of God. We have no more right to inquire why evil should be made to deter from evil, than to investigate into the origin of evil itself. Enough if we know and experience that the wages of sin is death; but we have here even more to consider. While we can have no doubt that the tragedy of Burke and Hare is calculated to deter not only from that sin which it involves, but from all those lesser ones which follow from the temptations of mammon, we have to recollect that it put an end to a pre-existing evil of gigantic magnitude, and which all the adjurations of a distressed people were not able otherwise to effect. That evil, as we have seen, was body-snatching. No sooner were the murders which the temptations of that practice induced brought to light, than our legislators took to their powers and duties, and righted the nation. They saved the affections of the heart without annulling the aspirations of the intellect, served the purpose of science in its remedial application to physical ills, without desecrating the temple where burned the light of the spirit, and through which these ills are felt.

FOOTNOTES:

[1] Scotland, with her open church-yards in secluded places,
groaned under this infliction for centuries. See "An Account of
the most horrid and unchristian actions of the Grave-makers
in Edinburgh, their raising and selling of the dead, abhorred by
Turks and heathens, found out in this present year, 1711, in the
month of May." We offer an extract:—

"Methink I hear the latter trumpet sound,
When emptie graves into this place is found,
Of young and old, which is most strange to me,
What kind of resurrection this may be.
I thought God had reserved this power alone
Unto Himself, till He erect'd His throne
Into the clouds with His attendants by,
That He might judge the world in equity;
But now I see the contrair in our land,
Since men do raise the dead by their own hand."

The price was known too, as a fixed thing apparently—

"As I'm inform'd the chirurgeons did give
Forty shillings for each one they receive."

[2] Take this specimen of his self-esteem:—"Gentlemen, I may
mention that I have already taught the science of anatomy to
about 5000 medical men now spread over the surface of the
earth, and some of these have turned out most remarkable
for their knowledge, genius, and originality, for they now
occupy some of the most conspicuous and trying positions in
Europe. As a piece of curious testimony to my capabilities of
communicating to you knowledge, I may venture to mention
to you an interesting fact which took place last summer
while on a visit to my distinguished friend and pupil, the

Right Honourable the Earl of Breadalbane, at his beautiful
and picturesque seat of Taymouth Castle, in the shire of
Perth. At a large party given by the noble Earl to the leading
nobility and gentry of Scotland, where, to use the beautiful
language of Byron,

'A thousand hearts beat happily, and when
Music arose with its voluptuous swell,
And all went merry as a marriage-bell;'

I, who was there as the Earl's guest, and knew personally none
of the noble Earl's distinguished personages of the party,
happened to fall accidentally into conversation with a noble
lord—an adjoining proprietor of our generous host's—on the
subject of the breeding of cattle; and, although our conversation
originated in the slightest possible observation, it went on
naturally enough, until, by imperceptible degrees, I was
forced to open up the whole extensive stores of my anatomical
and physiological knowledge, (especially the comparative
departments of these subjects,) and before I had addressed
myself to the noble lord for ten minutes continuously, for I
actually felt myself inspired by my situation, the whole beauty
and fashion of the large suite of rooms were surrounding me,
and seemed entranced with the deep thought that poured from
my lips. I naturally felt somewhat abashed that I had drawn
upon myself so much observation, but the direct and indirect
compliments that were paid to knowledge and eloquence amply
compensated for this painful sensation. Among other things,
I shall never forget the observation of an old, fashionable, and
distinguished dame, evidently belonging to the middle portion
of the last century, in these memorable words, 'He's a cunning
loon that, he would wile the lav'rock frae the lift,' for her quaint
remark seemed to embody, in few words, the entire sentiment of
the large and distinguished company, all illustrating the adage
of Bacon, that knowledge is power; and, when brought to bear

with eloquence and propriety, it affects equally all conditions of life with its mighty overwhelming strength."

[3] The following, extracted from the MS. notes of a student, may be taken as a specimen of Knox's mode of dealing with his brethren:-"Before commencing to-day's lecture, I am compelled by the sacred calls of duty to notice an extraordinary surgical operation which has this morning been performed in a neighbouring building by a gentleman [Mr Liston] who, I believe, regards himself as the first surgeon in Europe. A country labourer from the neighbourhood of Tranent came to the Infirmary a few days ago with an aneurism of considerable extent, connected with one of the large arteries of the neck; and, notwithstanding of its being obvious to the merest tyro that it was an aneurism, the most distinguished surgeon in Europe, after an apparently searching examination, pronounced it to be an abscess. Accordingly, this professional celebrity—who, among other things, plumes himself upon the wonderful strength of his hands and arms, without pretension to head, and is an amateur member of the ring—plunged his knife into what he thus foolishly imagined to be an abscess; and the blood, bursting forth from the deep gash in the aneurismal sac, the patient was dead in a few seconds. This notable member of the profession is actually an extra-academical lecturer on surgery in this great metropolis; and on this occasion was assisted by a gentleman similarly constituted, both intellectually and physically, who had been trained up under the fostering care of a learned professor in a certain university, who inherited his anatomical genius from his ancestors, and who has recently published a work on the anatomy of the human body, in which, among other notabilities, no notice is taken of the pericardium. Tracing the assistant of our distinguished operator further back, I have discovered that he had been originally apprenticed to a butcher of this city, but that he had been dismissed from this service for stealing a sheep's head and trotters from his

employer's shambles. It is surely unnecessary for me to add that a knowledge of anatomy, physiology, pathology, and surgery, is neither connected with nor dependent upon brute force, ignorance, and presumption; nor has it anything to do with an utter destitution of honour and common honesty."—(Roars of applause, mixed with a few hisses.)

[4] However little connexion there seems between our indifference as to what becomes of the body and our belief in the immortality of the soul, it is, nevertheless, certain that believers and unbelievers do not view the subject in the same light. The ancients, in spite of Aristotle, (as we find him construed by Pomponatius,) were greater *natural* believers in the doctrine of the soul's immortality, than the moderns, in spite of Des Cartes. And see how they venerated the dead! The Athenians put to death six generals who had achieved for them the greatest of their victories, because they had omitted to bury those who had been killed. When Alcyoneus took the head of Pyrrhus to his father Antigonus, that king struck the bearer with a staff, covered his eyes, and wept, and ordered that the dead body and the head should be honourably put on the pyre. The rabbinical fable of the *Luz*, or little bone of the size of a grain, which could not be destroyed even by fire, and from which *nostrum corpus animate repullulascet*, seems to have spread beyond Judea. We need not speak of Egypt and its sacred mummies.

[5] If, in these narratives, it may be found that I depart in some details from the discrepant confessions of Burke, I have to plead such authority as I possess, in a collection of notes taken at the time by one who intended to use them in a fuller account than that comprised in the two pamphlets published by Buchanan.

[6] She had been once a lodger in Log's house.

[7] On examining the animal, the knackers found that many old sores become hollows had been filled up with tow, and then plastered over with a thin skin.

[8] They are fully described, for the first time we believe, in "Curiosities of Crime in Edinburgh."

[9] We adopt this version in preference to another, which substitutes Burke.

[10] It was never believed that the cases confessed to by Burke exhausted the real list. One in particular, that of a little Italian boy, Ludovico, who went about with white mice, was a favourite story which could not be doubted, when it was known that the people of Tanner's Close saw, for years afterwards, the two little animals haunting the dark recesses, where their young master had been sacrificed. And many other visions were seen there besides those of the white mice. But, apart from these superstitions, it is certain that there was found in Hare's house a cage with the mice's turning-wheel in it, which clearly had belonged to one of these Italian wanderers. The silence of Burke on the subject is of no importance, for his confessions did not agree, and, besides, it was properly asked, might not poor Ludovico have been the subject which Hare managed "on his own hook" unknown to Burke? Like the others, he would be mourned, but it would be far away in some little hamlet among the Apennines.

[11] A subscription was raised for Gray. He had saved the lives of probably a score of men and women; but so poorly was he remunerated, that he did not get a pound a head for these *lives*, or a tenth of that got by Burke for his *bodies*.

[12] The fury against the doctors ran so high not only in Edinburgh, but in Dumfries, that they were exposed to the risk of the

fate they experienced under Cato the Censor:—"Romani quondam, sub Catone Censorio, medicos omnes et urbe tota et tota Italia pepulerunt eorum funesta mendacia crudelitatemque aversati."—*Agrippa de Van. Scien.* cap. 83. See, too, Montaigne:—"Les Romains avaient este six cens ans avant que de recevoir la médecine; mais après l'avoir essayée, ils la chassèrent de leur ville par entremise de Caton le Censeur." This proscription of doctors lasted to the time of the first emperors; but even if they had been tolerated, the national reverence for the dead would have been an effectual bar to such practices as Scotland groaned under for centuries. We are not left to wonder how they contrived to keep the body right in these ancient times, for we know that Cato purged his household; and Horace lets us up to the knowledge the old women had of simples.

[13] The allusion is to Knox. His house was afterwards surrounded by a furious mob, who smashed his windows, and he was obliged to secrete himself for a time.

[14] The entire Parliament Square rang as by the echoes of a jubilee.

[15] The story that the cancerous affection arose from the saliva of Daft Jamie, communicated by a bite, was resolutely held to by the people.

[16] "He struggled a good deal," says an eye-witness, who was very near, "and put out his legs as if to catch something with his feet; but some of the undertaker's men, who were below the drop, took him by the feet, and sent him spinning round,—a motion which was continued until he was drawn up above the level of the scaffold."

[17] An eye-witness, whose notes we have, says, "He (Burke) was one of the most symmetrical men I ever saw, finely-developed muscles, and finely-formed, of the athlete class."

[18] "After this exhibition," says an eye-witness, "Burke was cut up and put in pickle for the lecture-table. He was cut up in quarters, or rather portions, and salted, and, with a strange aptness of poetical justice, put into barrels. At that time an early acquaintance and school-fellow was assistant to the professor, and with him I frequently visited the dissecting-room, when calling on him at his apartments at the College. He is now a physician in the Carse of Gowrie. He shewed me Burke's remains, and gave me the skin of his *neck* and of the right arm. These I had *tanned*—the neck brown, and the arm white. The white was as pure as white kid, but as thick as white sheepskin; and the brown was like brown tanned sheepskin. It was curious that the mark of the rope remained on the leather after being tanned. Of that neck-leather I had a tobacco-doss made; and on the white leather of the right arm I got Johnston to print the portraits of Burke and his wife, and Hare, which I gave to the noted antiquarian and collector of curiosities, Mr Fraser, jeweller, and it was in one of his cases for many years—may be still, if he is alive."

[19] The portraits of Burke and M'Dougal were got by the artist's having been introduced into the judges' private room, behind the bench. To complete the group, Mr Johnston, the engraver, managed through the governor to get an artist into the passage between the airing-grounds, when Hare was taking his walk. Hare saw the party sketching, came right up to the iron grating, and stood like a soldier at attention, until the sketch was completed. He then said, "Now, sir, peetch me a shilling for that."

[20] For much of what follows of Hare's flight we are indebted to the pencil-pen of Mr M'Diarmid of the *Dumfries Courier*.

[21] We might, perhaps, say, except till now. Not long ago, we were told by a lady, who was in Paris about the year 1859, that,

having occasion for a nurse, she employed a woman, apparently between sixty and seventy years of age. She gave her name as Mrs Hare, and upon being questioned whether she had been ever in Scotland, she denied it, stating that she came from Ireland. Yet she often sung Scotch songs; and what brings out the suspicion that she was the real Mrs Hare the more is, that she had a daughter, whose age, over thirty, agrees perfectly with that of the infant she had in her arms when in court. In addition to all this, the woman's face was just that of the picture published at the time.

[22] After Burke's execution, M'Dougal is said to have made a wonderful revelation. One night, when the two men were deep in an orgy, Burke put the question, "What they would do when they could get no more bodies?" to which Hare answered, "That they could never be absolutely at a loss while their two wives remained, but that would only be when they were hard up." The conversation had been overheard by one of the women.

Made in the USA
Columbia, SC
14 April 2023

15362728R00138